BIOTECHNOLOGY

IN FOCUS

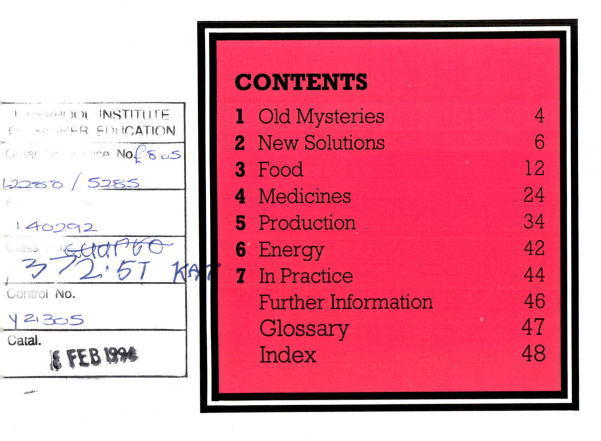

CONTENTS

1 Old Mysteries — 4

2 New Solutions — 6

3 Food — 12

4 Medicines — 24

5 Production — 34

6 Energy — 42

7 In Practice — 44

Further Information — 46

Glossary — 47

Index — 48

This edition published 1990 by
Franklin Watts
96 Leonard Street
London EC2A 4RH

ISBN 0 7496 0325 9

Original edition published 1988 by
Hobsons Publishing plc
Produced in conjunction with and sponsored by
Lilly Industries and its associated companies
Elanco Products, Dista Products and Eli Lilly

A CIP catalogue record for this book is
available from the British Library

Editor: Dr Melanie Quin
Consultant Editor: Dr W T Mason
Design: Ken Vail Studios
Designer: Pete Burclaff
Art Direction: Sally Moon
Graphics and illustrations by: Michael Badrocke, Paul
Cookson, Peter Covill, John Erwood, Line and Line, Malcolm Ryan

Acknowledgements
We are grateful to the following for supplying photographic
material:

pp 4/5   Eden Vale; The Victoria Wine Company Ltd; Michael
            Fogden/OSF; Doug Allen/OSF
p 6   Dr A Lesk, Laboratory of Molecular Biology/Science
            Photo Library
pp 8/9   Lever Brothers Ltd; The Brewers' Society

pp 10/11   Lilly Industries Ltd; The Mansell Collection; St Mary's
            Hospital Medical School/SPL; J W Watts, John Innes
            Institute; Dr M G K Jones, Dr N Fish/Rothamsted
p 15   Dr R Angold, RHM Research and Engineering Ltd;
            Marlow Foods Ltd; Bovril Ltd
pp 16/17   British Meat; AFRC Institute of Animal Physiology,
            Cambridge (Frosty II, chimaera); Animal Biotechnology
            Cambridge Ltd/AFRC Institute of Animal Physiology and
            Genetics Research, Cambridge (Microinjection)
pp 18/19   AFRC Institute of Animal Physiology, Cambridge
pp 20/21   Flour Advisory Bureau Ltd; Danish Dairy Board
pp 22/23   Photo Library International
pp 24/25   Bernard Pierre Wolff/SPL; J Broek/Biozentrum, University
            of Basel/SPL
p 26   Child Growth Foundation
p 29   Lilly Industries Ltd
pp 30/31   M T Scott, Wellcome Biotech; Genetics International UK
pp 32/33   Associated Press
p 35   The Boots Company plc
pp 36/37   Imperial Chemical Industries plc
p 39   Dr W J Ingledew/SPL; B A Whitton, Department of
            Botany, University of Durham
pp 40/41   Photo Library International; Water Authorities
            Association
pp 42/43   Paulo Fridman/Colorific!; Farming Information Centre
p 45   Leicester Biocentre

We also acknowledge the following sources of information:

p 9   Table after Higgins, I J in *Biotechnology: Principles and
            Applications* ed. I J Higgins, D J Best, J Jones Ch. 1 p. 19,
            Blackwell Scientific Publications (1985)
pp 22/23   Illustration after Holland, T and Bore, A, *French Wines*,
            MacDonald Guidelines series, MacDonald Educational
            (1978) pp 28/29
p 25   Illustration after McKean, D G, *GCSE Biology*, John
            Murray (1986) p 313
p 26   Graph supplied by Dr N D Barnes, Addenbrooke's
            Hospital
p 44   Extract reprinted by permission from *Nature* Vol. 250,
            July 19 1974 p. 175 Copyright © Macmillan Magazines
            Limited.

BIOTECHNOLOGY
IN FOCUS

Jonathan Katz and Dr David B Sattelle

FRANKLIN WATTS

LONDON • NEW YORK • SYDNEY • TORONTO

1: OLD MYSTERIES

Biotechnology may look a long and complicated word, but it simply describes the way we use plant and animal cells and microbes to produce substances that are useful to mankind.

Common products of biotechnology include yoghurt and a variety of alcoholic drinks.

The Ploughman's Lunch

Although the word 'biotechnology' is new, the subject it describes has an ancient history. For thousands of years, we have been making **beer**, **wine** and bread, preserving food by turning milk into yoghurt and cheese, and by bottling and pickling food in vinegar. So, look at a ploughman's lunch: bread, butter, cheese, pickle and beer are all products of biotechnology.

Biotechnology is all around us, every day, just as it was with our ancestors many years ago. The only difference is that it is no longer mysterious. We now understand how biotechnology works and can use it to produce a huge variety of materials, from fuels to medicines, from new crop plants to healthier animals and from chemicals to plastics.

MICROBES: THE NEW INDUSTRIAL GIANTS SEEN ONLY UNDER THE MICROSCOPE

The smallest division on your ruler is 1 mm. Imagine that divided up into 1000 equal segments. Each one of these *very* small segments is a micron and this is the scale we need to use to measure microbes, many of which we could never see without a microscope.

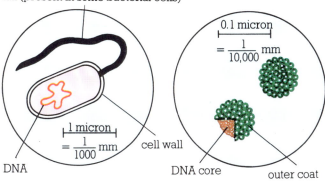

tail (present in some bacterial cells)

0.1 micron $= \frac{1}{10,000}$ mm

1 micron $= \frac{1}{1000}$ mm

cell wall

DNA

DNA core

outer coat

Bacterium

Virus

All living organisms are made up of **cells**. The word **microbe** usually means a very small living thing (such as a bacterium) that has only one cell. We shall use it to include single-cell plants, animals and moulds. **Viruses** are even smaller than bacteria and are not true cells – they are rather more like crystals. They can only reproduce themselves when inside cells.

virus particles

cell nucleus containing DNA in chromosomes

cell wall

1 micron

1 micron

cell cytoplasm

A bacterium infected with a virus.

Yeast cells

The real stars of biotechnology are the microbes that do all the work. These tiny **organisms**, thousands of which can fit onto the head of a pin, are amazingly versatile and can be found almost everywhere – some microbes can live in boiling water or frozen in ice. Others can feed on wood, plastic, petrol and even solid rock.

The reason biotechnology has become so exciting in recent years is because of **genetic engineering**. The offspring of living organisms are similar to their parents. These likenesses can be passed on through generations and are said to be heritable or genetic. Genetic engineering describes the way in which scientists can alter the genetic make-up of an organism by introducing new molecules of heredity (**DNA**) to the DNA already present and tightly packaged as **chromosomes** in the nucleus of living cells. The DNA is like a coded message that scientists have now deciphered. Using genetic engineering (or manipulation) scientists can insert totally foreign pieces of DNA into microbes and so make the microbes produce a useful substance.

Some microbes can thrive in the most unlikely surroundings, including the icy wastes of Antarctica and hot springs.

Millions of different organisms inhabit the Earth, but they are all made up of cells. Cells are the basic units of life, and they are very small. It would take 5000 human red blood cells to cover the dot on the letter i.

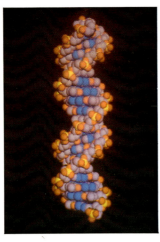

This picture, produced by a computer, shows clearly the double-helix structure of DNA.

Messages in Code

Large organisms are made up of hundreds of different types of cells, each with a special job. The cells of the eye can detect light. Muscle cells provide the power for movement. All the cells contribute to the well-being of the organism and each depends on the others for survival.

By contrast, most of the organisms that are of interest to the biotechnologist – the microbes – consist of only one cell. Each cell is independent and given appropriate conditions can perform all the functions it needs to survive and reproduce.

Although these cells are too small to see by eye, they can perform many thousands of different chemical reactions. The reactions do not all take place in a single step but in a number of small steps. These steps are controlled by **enzymes**. An enzyme is a biological catalyst – that is, a substance that speeds up a biological process and is unchanged by it.

DNA, Chromosomes and the Key to Life

If we look at cells dividing under a microscope, we can see long threads called chromosomes. These threads are made up of many tiny units called **genes**. Genes instruct our bodies to make **proteins** – the workhorse molecules of biology that give living cells all their diverse forms and functions. Each gene controls the production of a particular protein or enzyme. It is these, in turn, which are responsible for the characteristics of a particular cell or organism. Genes are the units of heredity passed on from one generation to the next.

Chromosomes and genes are made up of DNA. In 1953 scientists working at the University of Cambridge discovered the nature of DNA.

How a pancreas cell produces insulin.

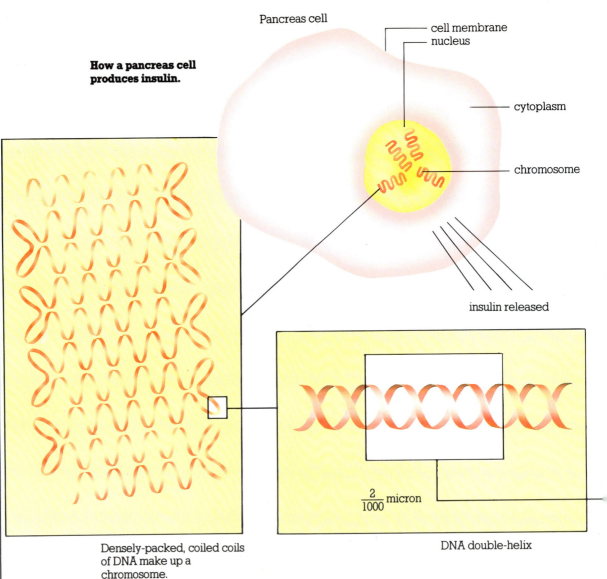

Pancreas cell

cell membrane
nucleus

cytoplasm

chromosome

insulin released

$\frac{2}{1000}$ micron

Densely-packed, coiled coils of DNA make up a chromosome.

DNA double-helix

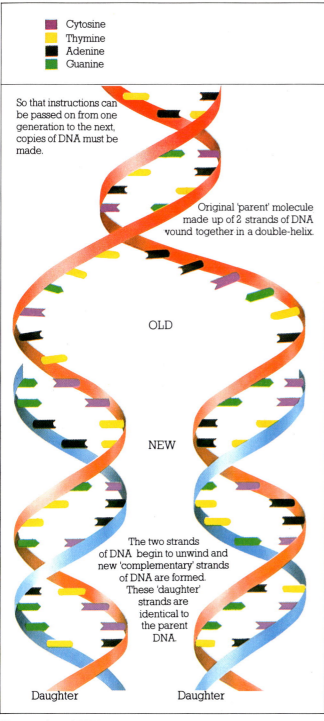

Cytosine
Thymine
Adenine
Guanine

So that instructions can be passed on from one generation to the next, copies of DNA must be made.

Original 'parent' molecule made up of 2 strands of DNA wound together in a double-helix.

OLD

NEW

The two strands of DNA begin to unwind and new 'complementary' strands of DNA are formed. These 'daughter' strands are identical to the parent DNA.

Daughter   Daughter

How copies of DNA are made.

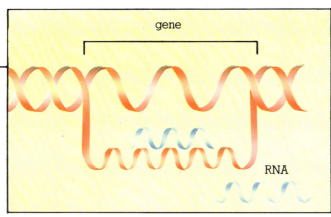

gene

RNA

A gene is that part of the DNA that codes for a protein, e.g. insulin. The code is copied as

RNA which acts as a template for insulin production.

A car is built from the engineer's drawing or 'blueprint'. DNA has been described as the 'blueprint for life' – it contains the plans of the cell and controls the way characteristics are passed on from one generation to the next. One such characteristic is eye colour. If you keep pets such as rabbits, cats or hamsters, do you see similarities between the different generations?

Our understanding of the nature of DNA opened the way for genetic engineering.

Genetic engineering is very important to biotechnology because it can enable microbes to make products they would not normally make. Molecular biologists can transfer genes, made from DNA, from one type of cell to another completely different type of cell. For example, genes from human cells can be transferred to microbial cells. This causes the microbes to produce human proteins, for example **insulin** (see below and page 10).

Genetic engineering allows biotechnologists to produce new medicines, fuels, foods, plants, and animals!

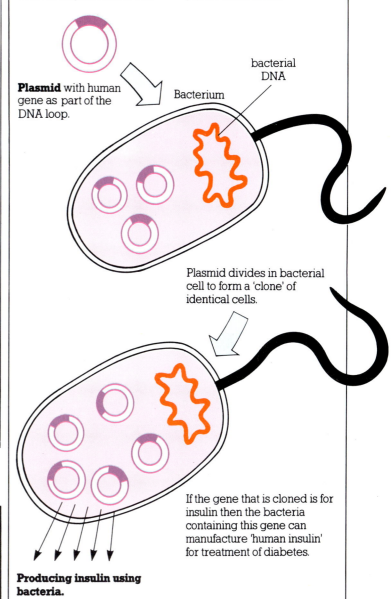

Plasmid with human gene as part of the DNA loop.

Bacterium

bacterial DNA

Plasmid divides in bacterial cell to form a 'clone' of identical cells.

If the gene that is cloned is for insulin then the bacteria containing this gene can manufacture 'human insulin' for treatment of diabetes.

Producing insulin using bacteria.

Looking at chromosomes
Cut off the tip of a young root and place in a watch glass of acidified acetic orcein stain. Warm the watchglass for 5 minutes. Put the root tip on a slide with a drop of stain. Break it up with a needle to spread out the cells. Put on a coverslip and look at your slide under low and then high power. Can you see the chromosomes?

A New Approach

The seeds of biotechnology are rooted deep in the past, but the fruits of its growth are here for us to pick now and in the future.

Biotechnology in the 20th century can be traced back to World War I when it was exploited by both Britain and Germany to produce chemicals to make explosives. Later, in World War II, biotechnology came to the rescue in the production of **penicillin** for treating the wounded (see page 10). This formed the basis for today's massive **antibiotics** industry.

When fuel is expensive or in short supply, microbes can be used to make fuel-alcohol from starch. This process was exploited before the rise of the petrochemical industry in the 1950s and 1960s. The huge increase in the price of oil in the early 1970s made the process popular again, especially in countries such as Brazil.

The Bio-Industrial Revolution

The development of genetic engineering in the 1970s really got the ball rolling for what has been called the bio-industrial revolution.

Many of the important developments in biotechnology have come from work in Britain, such as the discovery of DNA and **monoclonal antibodies**.

Do you know why certain washing powders are referred to as 'biological'? This is because they contain enzymes. How do you think adding enzymes can improve the actions of a washing powder?

NEW

BIOLOGICAL
BLUE

Lever
3.1 Kg

Surf

AUTOMATIC

So clean you can smell it's clean

Washday enzymes.

Unfortunately, it is not always the countries which invent new technology that reap its benefits. The USA and Japan are in the best position now, but we in Britain and Europe are not too far behind.

Biotechnology has expanded in different ways around the world. In the USA dozens of small firms have set up in the last ten years. Many of them have considerable expertise and they receive huge sums of money from venture capitalists and multi-national corporations. Large sums of money have also been put into basic research in universities.

In Japan the government provides the backing for biotechnology. Japanese scientists have made great strides in fermentation technology and have a large and successful trade in some **amino acids**, enzymes and food additives. Japan already earns over £30 billion a year from exploiting microbes.

Britain has a strong reputation for research in the biological sciences. This research is now being exploited, via both small start-up companies and large multi-national ones. This is actively encouraged by the government.

Biotechnology is now poised to become a major industry both in Britain and in the rest of the world.

PRODUCT	ESTIMATED WORLD MARKET BY THE YEAR 2000 (MILLIONS OF POUNDS)
Chemicals	9000
Energy	12000
Food	12000
Medicine	8000
Miscellaneous (e.g. pollution monitoring and control, plastics, mineral leaching)	15000
TOTAL	56000

This table shows estimates of the likely world markets for products of the 'new biotechnology' by the year 2000.

Beer is produced in this modern biotechnology-based factory.

Investigating biological washing powder
Plan and carry out an experiment to see how well 'biological' washing powder gets rid of stains like blood, egg and mud compared with 'ordinary' washing powder. Remember to make your experiment 'fair'. What do you find?

Penicillin and Insulin – Biotechnology Products Saving Lives

As with many great scientific discoveries, the history of penicillin involves an element of luck. It triggered the birth of modern biotechnology.

In 1928, Alexander Fleming was working in his laboratory at St Mary's Hospital in London. One day in September, he noticed that a petri dish had been contaminated with a mould. What really caught his attention was the fact that no bacteria had grown around the mould. He reasoned, correctly, that the mould had produced some substance which stopped the bacteria growing. He called this substance penicillin after the mould, *Penicillium notatum*.

Strangely, Fleming did not follow up his findings. He did perform a few experiments, and showed that the substance was not harmful to mice. But he did not try to purify it any further, or to test its effect on infected mice. We should remember that no single scientist can make such a discovery *and* turn it into a drug that is available worldwide. To do that needs lots of different skills.

Alexander Fleming (1881–1955).

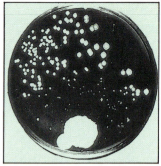

A photograph of the original culture plate of the mould *Penicillium notatum* from which Fleming 'discovered' penicillin. The *Penicillium* mould at the bottom is releasing penicillin into the surroundings and this has stopped the bacteria growing near it. The light blobs towards the top and left are colonies of bacteria growing untouched by the penicillin.

In the human body, insulin is produced by the pancreas and goes directly into the bloodstream. Now human insulin can also be made by genetically-engineered bacteria.

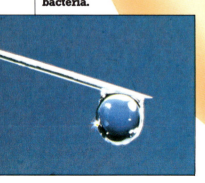

Vein

Main d

Part of digestive system

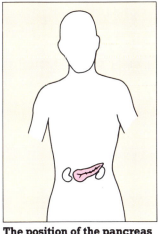

The position of the pancreas in the body.

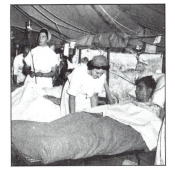

Penicillin was used to treat wounded soldiers during World War II. Many of the soldiers were nursed in field hospitals, like this one in Normandy, France.

In the early days of penicillin production, laboratory flasks were used. Nowadays large-scale production facilities are needed to meet the demand for modern antibiotics. The photograph shows antibiotic extraction equipment at Dista Products Ltd.

w of insulin
loodstream

Pancreas

Teamwork Produces the Answer

In World War II (1939–45) there was an urgent need to produce an effective antibiotic in large quantities to treat the wounded. This need brought together scientists and technologists to develop a production process. Three main questions had to be answered:

1. Which is the best type of mould?
2. How can penicillin be separated from other substances that the mould produces?
3. What is the best design of apparatus to grow the mould and to extract the penicillin?

In all, 700 scientists in thirty laboratories took part. By 1944 there was enough penicillin to treat all the seriously injured British, American and Allied Forces casualties during the invasion of Europe. Even then, the process was still only a slight scale-up of the flasks used by two other key scientists in penicillin development, Howard Florey and Ernst Chain.

Since the war, penicillin production has grown into a massive industrial process. The variety of mould now used produces a far greater yield of penicillin.

Scientists now use other types of organisms to produce different antibiotics, like the **cephalosporins** used for patients having liver, kidney or heart transplants and to control a variety of other infections. The cephalosporins were discovered initially in mould growing near a sewage outlet in Italy.

Insulin – From Animals or Bacteria To Humans

Insulin is another very important protein that has a special job to do in our bodies – to allow the cells of the body to take up the sugars that build up in our blood after eating such foods as bread and potatoes.

Insulin is made in the **pancreas**. Some people cannot make enough insulin to keep their blood sugar at the right level; they suffer from a disease called *diabetes mellitus*. In this country, on average, 2 people in every 100 suffer from diabetes. Some diabetics (people who suffer from diabetes) can keep their blood sugar levels under control by being careful to eat foods that contain very little or no sugar. But others who are not so lucky, about 1 in 3 of all diabetics, must inject themselves with insulin.

In the past, the only available insulin for diabetics was extracted from the pancreas of pigs or cows. Now, by using genetic engineering, scientists can modify bacteria so that they can produce human insulin. In fact, insulin produced in this way by Eli Lilly & Company was the very first genetically-engineered protein to be given to humans.

Human insulin produced in this way has a number of advantages over insulin extracted from cows or pigs.

1. Pork and beef insulin differ in structure from human insulin and in some patients stimulate an allergic response. Genetically-engineered insulin, on the other hand, has exactly the same composition as human insulin, so the allergic response is significantly less.
2. As the number of diabetics in the world increases, the supply of animal pancreases cannot keep up with the demand for insulin – genetically-engineered insulin can be produced in any quantity required to meet the needs of known patients.
3. Some people do not like injecting themselves with insulin that comes from animals.

Human insulin being injected into a volunteer at Guy's Hospital, London during the first human trial of Lilly's genetically-engineered product.

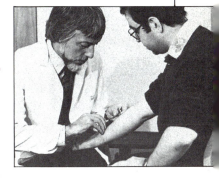

11

3: FOOD

In a world where the population is growing by millions every year, feeding everybody is a problem which is becoming more and more difficult to solve. With the aid of biotechnology, scientists can produce new strains of plants where once there would have been little hope of a successful harvest.

Animal diseases can be controlled by biotechnology. As a result of genetic engineering, cows can produce more milk and leaner meat.

In the very near future microbes will be a major source of nourishment. In an ever-growing world, biotechnology is making rapid advances towards solving the food problem.

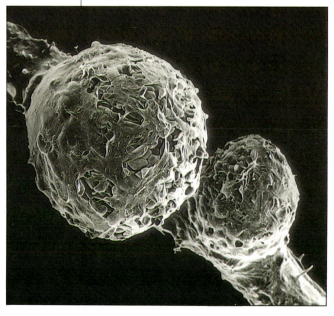

An electron micrograph of root nodules on a pea plant. These are caused by the nitrogen-fixing bacteria.

Improving crop plants

For generations, farmers have been selecting and breeding crop plants to produce more food. Today, genetic engineering gives agricultural scientists a valuable new tool. They hope, soon, to produce plants that can live in places where the climate does not normally allow plants to survive. It may be too cold, for example, and microbes that prevent ice formation on plants have been developed. We may also have plants that can produce their own fertilisers and resist the attacks of insects and viruses.

Plants need nitrogen to build up vital components inside their cells, such as proteins and DNA. Animals can obtain their nitrogen by eating plants or other animals, but plants get their nitrogen from the soil. Although air contains about 80% nitrogen and about 20% oxygen, for most forms of life nitrogen gas is useless. Only when it is 'fixed' in the form of ammonia (NH_3) or nitrates can it be used by plants for growth. This process is called **nitrogen fixation**.

Farmers can add nitrogen fertilisers to the soil, but this is expensive. And when it rains some of the fertiliser is washed into rivers causing pollution, including unwanted growth of microscopic water plants such as algae.

Peas, beans and clover have been known since Roman times to restore fertility to soil where a crop such as wheat had previously grown. We now know that this is because millions of bacteria live in the root nodules of these plants. The bacteria take nitrogen directly from the air and 'fix' it into a form that plants can use for growth.

Food crops such as soya beans and peanuts can also fix nitrogen from the air but unfortunately cereals like wheat and barley cannot. Scientists are using genetic engineering to alter these nitrogen-fixing bacteria so that they will be able to live in the roots of cereals and act as a built-in fertiliser factory.

Genetic engineering is also being explored as a way to improve the food value of plants to make them more nutritious to eat.

Plant cells, unlike animal cells, have a thick, rigid cell wall. If this wall is dissolved using enzymes, we are left with a plant cell without its 'jacket' called a protoplast. Protoplasts from cells of different plants can be joined (fused together) to form a new plant called a 'hybrid'.

Potato and tomato plants have been joined in this way to form a 'pomato' plant. It is not that scientists are particularly fond of red chips, rather that they are trying to understand how plants function and how crops can be improved. This only works because the tomato

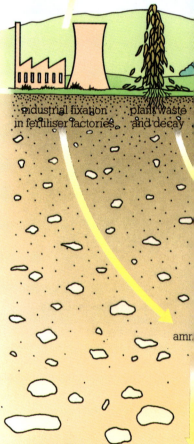

nitrogen gas in the air

industrial fixation in fertiliser factories

plant waste and decay

amr.

The Nitrogen Cycle. The fixing of nitrogen by bacteria in root nodules is only one stage in this complex process.

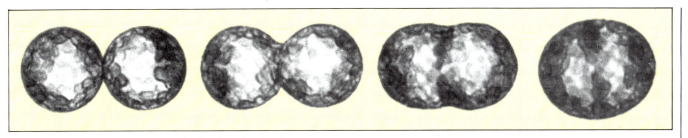

Two tobacco protoplasts (cells with their cell walls removed) in the process of fusing to form a single cell.

and the potato belong to the same family of plants. A 'wheatabbage' (wheat crossed with cabbage) would not be so easy to construct.

Some types of plant cell can grow a whole plant from just the one cell. This is very useful for plant breeders since it means that thousands of identical plants (or clones) can be grown from the cell of a single plant that has been selected. For example, hundreds of healthy clones can be produced starting from a single plant that is free from a particular plant disease.

This can readily be achieved for a number of vegetables, including carrots and potatoes, as well as for ornamental plants such as orchids.

Food for the Future
We can look forward to a future in which it will be possible to grow plants that can resist disease and grow in parts of the world where people have gone hungry because the crops they planted could not stand the lack of water, or the heat. In this way biotechnology will help to feed the people of Sudan and Ethiopia.

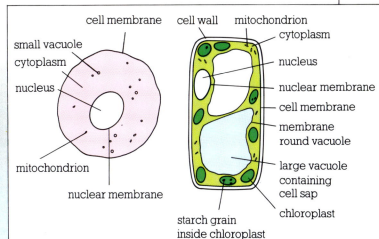

cell membrane
small vacuole
cytoplasm
nucleus
mitochondrion
nuclear membrane

cell wall
cytoplasm
nucleus
nuclear membrane
cell membrane
membrane round vacuole
large vacuole containing cell sap
chloroplast
starch grain inside chloroplast

A typical animal cell (left) and plant cell as seen with a light microscope. Note the cell wall present in the plant cell but not in the animal cell.

The picture below shows three potato plants. The one on the left is a normal potato plant, which produces the potatoes we eat. The one on the right is a wild potato plant and it is resistant to a virus called the Potato Leaf Roll Virus. The plant in the centre has been produced by fusion of protoplasts from the two other plants. It has all the good points of the normal potato plant *and* resistance to Leaf Roll Virus.

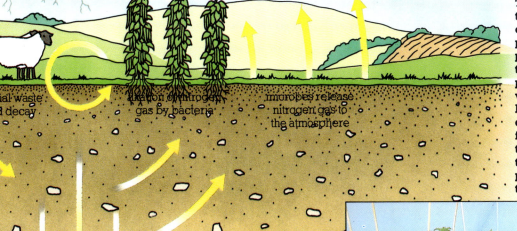

fixation by lightning

protein

animal waste and decay

fixation of nitrogen gas by bacteria

microbes release nitrogen gas to the atmosphere

nitrate (NO₃)

...hing of nitrogen compounds into the earth

Taking shoot cuttings
Using a healthy geranium or busy lizzie, cut a 5–10 cm shoot from just above a pair of leaves. Take off the lower leaves so that about 3 cm of stem are bare. Put into water (keeping the leaves clear). Leave for 2–3 weeks, changing the water every 3 days and feeding when roots form.

Edible Microbes

The thought of eating microbes may seem strange, but in fact we already eat lots of microbes, such as yeast extract (like Marmite), and foods containing microbes, such as cheese.

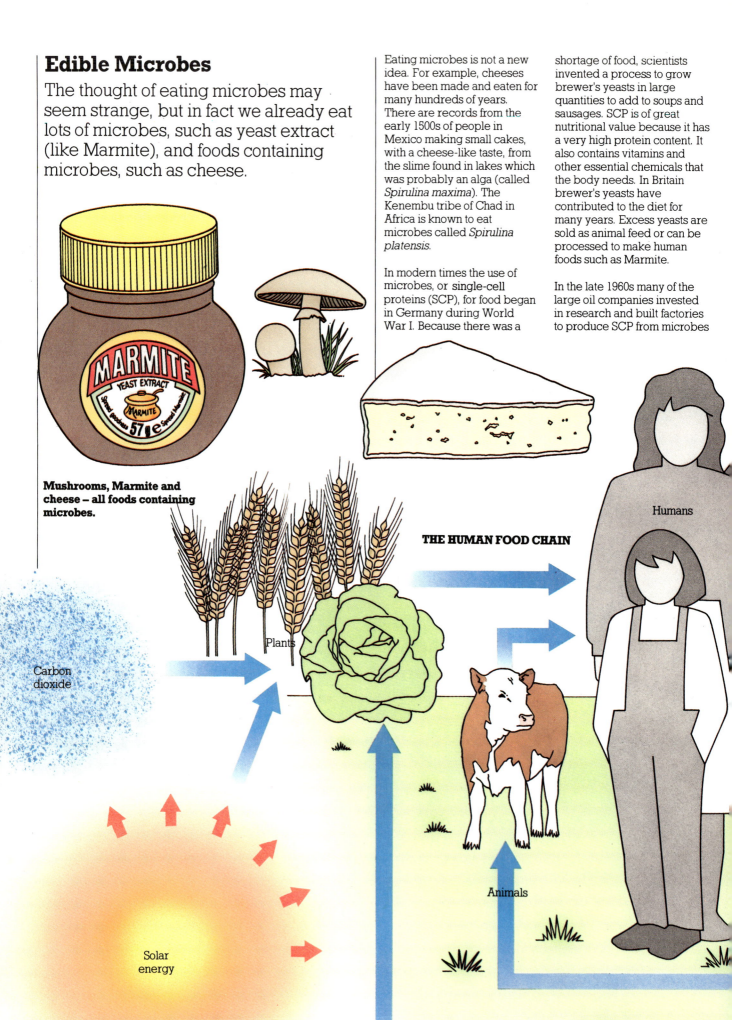

Mushrooms, Marmite and cheese – all foods containing microbes.

Eating microbes is not a new idea. For example, cheeses have been made and eaten for many hundreds of years. There are records from the early 1500s of people in Mexico making small cakes, with a cheese-like taste, from the slime found in lakes which was probably an alga (called *Spirulina maxima*). The Kenembu tribe of Chad in Africa is known to eat microbes called *Spirulina platensis*.

In modern times the use of microbes, or single-cell proteins (SCP), for food began in Germany during World War I. Because there was a shortage of food, scientists invented a process to grow brewer's yeasts in large quantities to add to soups and sausages. SCP is of great nutritional value because it has a very high protein content. It also contains vitamins and other essential chemicals that the body needs. In Britain brewer's yeasts have contributed to the diet for many years. Excess yeasts are sold as animal feed or can be processed to make human foods such as Marmite.

In the late 1960s many of the large oil companies invested in research and built factories to produce SCP from microbes

THE HUMAN FOOD CHAIN

Humans

Carbon dioxide

Plants

Solar energy

Animals

feeding on oil. Their aim was to produce cheap sources of protein that could be fed to animals or even to man. Whilst the idea was a very good one, the massive increase in the price of oil in the 1970s made these ventures financial failures. Also, there was much debate as to whether this type of protein would be suitable for human consumption.

Food from Gas

Some companies have persevered with SCP. ICI, for example, have produced an animal food called Pruteen by

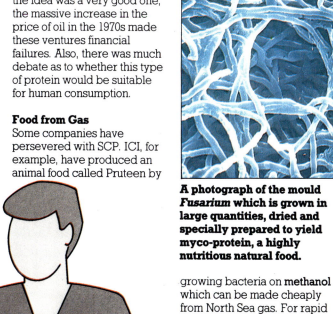

A photograph of the mould *Fusarium* which is grown in large quantities, dried and specially prepared to yield myco-protein, a highly nutritious natural food.

growing bacteria on **methanol** which can be made cheaply from North Sea gas. For rapid growth, the bacteria are supplied with water, ammonia, mineral salts and air. They also need warmth. Conditions must be sterile so that no other microbes are present. This is

easier said than done as the growth vessel used is one of the largest in the world – the size of a block of flats.

A 'continuous culture' process can be used in the manufacture of Pruteen. Once the process is started the bacteria reproduce rapidly. Bacteria are continuously removed and replaced with starting materials. As a result the process can continue for up to six months.

Other companies are working

The range of savoury pies with fillings of 'Quorn' myco-protein.

on ways of producing high-protein foods for humans. Rank Hovis McDougall have invented a process for producing large quantities of a mould (*Fusarium*) which contains 45% protein and 13% fat, and is high in fibre. This 'myco-protein' is as nutritious as some types of meat.

An exciting prospect for the future is that of using waste products from industry as a source of nutrients for the production of SCP. In Sweden, biotechnologists have invented a process which uses the waste from paper-making mills to grow SCP which can then be used for animal feed.

In developing countries, SCP could be a low-technology solution to some of the food shortage problems. By growing *Spirulina* in lakes the yield of food could be as much as ten times greater per hectare than the yield of wheat. The protein content would be many times greater than for wheat.

SCP is tasteless and so can easily be modified into a variety of appetising foods by adding natural flavourings.

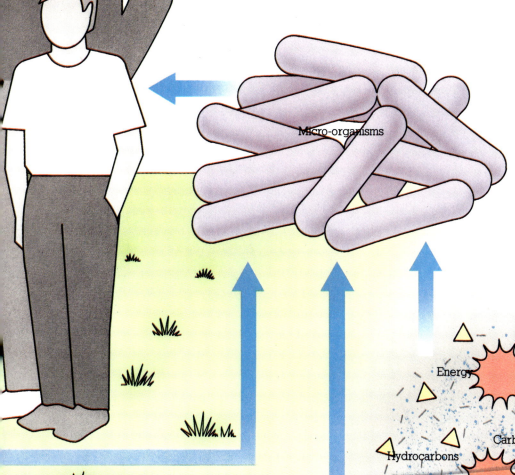

Micro-organisms

Energy

Carbon dioxide

Hydrocarbons

Healthier Animals

In the farmyard and milking shed, biotechnology may soon be giving us healthier and more productive domestic animals. In the wild, rare animal species may be saved from extinction by storing their eggs and sperm at very low temperatures.

Scientists have shown that when a cow is given a naturally-occurring substance called Bovine Somatotropin (BST), it can produce more milk for us to drink. In fact the cow can produce nearly 25% more milk than a cow that has not been given BST. Bacteria can now be genetically engineered to produce BST (once known as bovine growth hormone). Leaner, more wholesome meat is also the result of hormone treatment of cattle.

Vaccines to protect animals against disease have already been produced by genetic engineering. Some scientists in America were trying to think of new ways to control the **parasites** that live in the digestive systems of cattle.

They had almost given up when a soil sample was found to contain a tiny mould that produced the best ever worming agent. It is now used to control more than one kind of animal parasite. Rather than have chemists copy the 'natural' chemical it was easier to grow lots of microbes and let them do the complicated chemistry. In future, when your pet has treatment for 'worms' from the vet, the main ingredients might be made by biotechnology.

Biotechnology can also be used to save rare animals that face extinction. This may involve storage at low temperature of unfertilised eggs and sperm. Also by taking the fertilised eggs and embryos from a rare female

Treatment of cattle with hormones results in leaner, more wholesome meat.

'Frosty II', the world's first calf produced from a frozen embryo, was born in 1973. The technique is widely used for export of embryos and for long-term preservation of valuable genetic material.

Scientists who carry out research to produce healthier animals must be skilled in a number of techniques.

This animal, born at the Animal Research Station in Cambridge, is a cross between a sheep and a goat – a sheep/goat chimaera.

animal and cooling these down carefully to very low temperatures it is possible to store them for long periods of time. They are then put back inside a mother animal called a surrogate which can give birth to those offspring even years after the 'original' mother has died. Using this idea it is possible for a mother

of one species to give birth to offspring of another species. For example, a zebra foal has been born to a horse, and kids (baby goats) have been born to sheep. Using genetic engineering it is even possible to produce animals that are crosses between two species, called chimaeras.

But why do scientists want to use such techniques in the first place? It is not to make 'freakish' animals, but to make it easier for doctors to treat those with serious illnesses. For instance, work at the Animal Breeding Research Organisation in Scotland is producing 'transgenic' lambs, each bearing a human gene.

Foreign genes can be introduced into an organism by micro-injection of DNA. This picture shows micro-injection of a pig egg with foreign DNA. Genetic manipulation by such 'gene transfer' will have major applications in animal breeding, the pharmaceutical industry and biological research.

The lambs don't look or behave like humans, but they do make a very rare substance found in humans, and critical to our survival. This is called Factor 8, a protein which helps blood to clot. A flock of 100 such lambs could produce, in their body fluids, enough human blood-clotting protein to supply everyone in Europe suffering from the disease of haemophilia – a condition in which the blood fails to clot properly when the skin is cut. Other research is trying to use the same technique to produce a substance to help those with emphysema – a disease of the lungs resulting in breathing difficulties and most commonly started by smoking cigarettes.

These five lambs, born at the AFRC Animal Research Station, Cambridge, are the largest clone yet produced of a domestic farm animal. They are genetically identical.

Bread and Cheese

Making bread and cheese, and brewing beer, were the first examples of biotechnology and date back thousands of years. The processes must have been discovered by accident and were passed on through the ages from generation to generation as an art rather than a science. That microbes were involved in many of these processes was not known until the 19th century. Today, the production of bread and cheeses in factories is highly mechanised and is well understood by scientists and biotechnologists.

There are probably more different kinds of bread available than ever before.

How bread is made.

Flour, water and yeast are mixed together to form a dough.

Enzymes in the flour turn some of the starch in the flour into sugar. The sugar is then fermented by the yeast and carbon dioxide is produced. This causes the dough to rise.

Bread

The microbes used in the making of bread are yeasts. The most important one is *Saccharomyces cerevisiae*. To make bread, flour and water are mixed together and yeast is added to make dough rise. Dough rises because enzymes in the flour turn some of the starch in the flour into sugar. This sugar is then rapidly fermented by the yeast. The vast majority of organisms require oxygen to breathe (respire). Anaerobic fermentation is a technique which enables some microbes to survive well for long periods under oxygen-free conditions. Under these conditions yeast produces carbon dioxide (CO_2), a gas, which becomes trapped as bubbles in the dough, making it rise. Alcohol is also produced but this is destroyed when the bread is baked.

When baked, the yeast is inactivated, the alcohol produced by fermentation is destroyed, and water is driven from the dough. The result is a product with a light cellular texture: bread.

Yeast produces changes in the texture and taste of the dough by changing its physical and chemical nature. This was discovered in the late 19th century by a German chemist who invented baking powder. Baking powder is a mixture of chemicals that produces CO_2. The inventor thought that baking powder would take over from yeast in the making of bread – but this has not happened because bread made with yeast still tastes better.

How cheese is made.

Cheese

Cheese making depends on a special group of microbes called lactic acid bacteria. They are normally found in milk and are the reason why milk goes sour. The souring of milk provides a means of preserving it. Cheese making probably started as a means of preserving milk which would otherwise be wasted.

Hard cheeses are ripened by lactic acid bacteria which grow throughout the cheese.

A variety of Danish soft cheeses. These have been ripened by moulds and yeast enzymes. The blue colour seen in three of the cheeses is due to the growth of moulds.

Soft cheeses are ripened by mould and enzymes from yeasts that grow on the surface of the cheese. Some microbes play a very specific role in the ripening of cheeses. For example the blue colour and the unique taste of Roquefort cheese is due to growth of a blue-coloured mould (*Penicillium roqueforti*) throughout the cheese. Swiss cheese contains holes because of a microbe that produces CO_2.

Cheeses can be kept for quite long periods of time because the lactic acid bacteria make the cheese acidic. This prevents the growth of most micro-organisms that might otherwise spoil the cheese.

The manufacture of cheese can be divided into three main steps:

The cow (or sometimes goat or sheep) produces the milk.

1. Bacteria are added to the milk to make it go sour. The bacteria convert the lactose sugar in the milk into lactic acid which makes the milk curdle.

2. Rennin (an enzyme from the stomach of calves) is added. Rennin breaks down the proteins in the milk so that a solid is formed (the curds). The liquid that is left over (the whey) is then drained off.

3. The curds which form the cheese are allowed to ripen and mature. Ripening is a very complicated process. It is very variable and depends on the type of cheese being made.

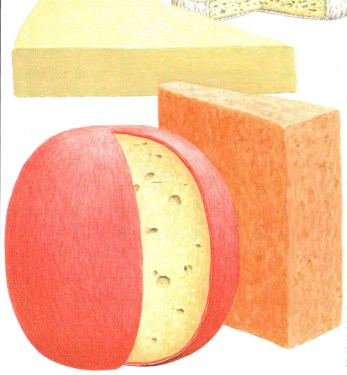

Watching rennet in action – making cheese
Rennet is a liquid which contains rennin – an enzyme. Add 1 part of rennet to 9 parts of milk in a test tube and mix the two together. Put into a water bath at 37 °C. Watch what happens. How long does the process take? What does the rennet do?

Wine and Beer

The people of the ancient civilisation of Babylon (whose capital city was on the Euphrates close to Baghdad in modern Iraq) probably 'invented' biotechnology when they brewed the first beer in 6000 BC. Brewing is a specialised type of fermentation which uses biotechnology to turn sugar into alcohol. Wine is also made by brewing and is mentioned in the Old Testament of the Bible.

These grapes will be used in the making of a red wine called Beaujolais.

Brewing depends on the fact that yeast cells can live without oxygen. They produce carbon dioxide (CO_2) and alcohol from sugar by a process called alcoholic fermentation.

White wine can be made from the sugary juices of both red and white grapes, but to make red wine the skins of red grapes are left in the wine. The alcohol in the wine draws out the red colour from the skins and this makes the wine red.

Some wines undergo a second spontaneous fermentation which is caused by lactic acid bacteria. This makes the wine less acidic.

Some special wines such as sparkling wines undergo further microbial fermentations. Sparkling wines have extra sugar added to them to make them undergo a second alcoholic fermentation which is under pressure. This produces CO_2 which is the cause of the bubbles.

Sherry is called a fortified wine because it has more alcohol than ordinary wine. This is the result of adding brandy during production.

The special taste of sherry is produced by exposing it to the air so that yeasts can grow on its surface. 'Dry' sherry is produced by allowing the yeast to develop fully. 'Sweet' sherry is produced when the yeast is less well developed.

Wine Making

This involves the fermentation of the sugars in grape juice into CO_2 and alcohol. After the grapes have been picked they are crushed in big vats to produce a raw juice called a must. This is very acidic and contains a large amount of sugar. The naturally occurring yeasts that grow on the grapes are usually all that is required to start the fermentation, although sometimes extra yeast needs to be added.

Fermentation takes place in a few days. The speed of the fermentation is controlled by temperature. Sometimes the wine must be cooled down to prevent it from getting too hot and killing the yeast.

When the fermentation is finished the new wine is cleared and stabilised before drinking. For a good red wine this process can take years.

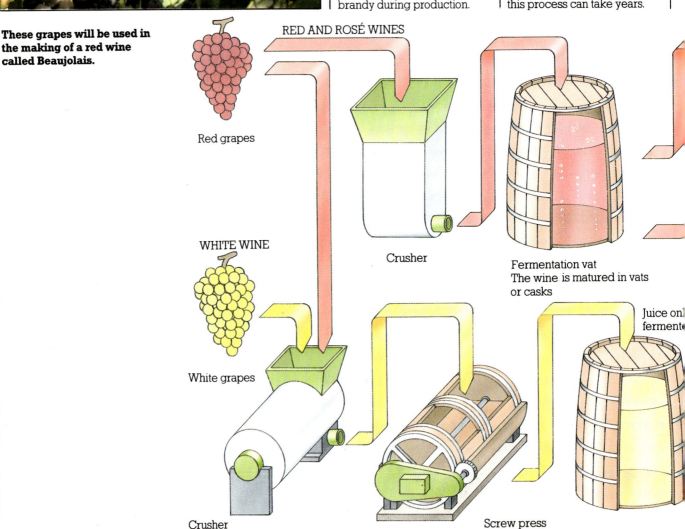

RED AND ROSÉ WINES

Red grapes

Crusher

Fermentation vat
The wine is matured in vats or casks

WHITE WINE

White grapes

Crusher

Screw press

Juice onl
fermente

Grapes for wine-making are grown in *vineyards*, like this one at Burgundy in France.

Beer Making

Beer is made from grain which, unlike grapes, contains only starch. The starch that is inside the grains must be converted into sugar before the grains can be fermented by yeasts. The grain most commonly used for making beer in Britain is barley.

Barley contains enzymes called amylases which are able to convert starch into sugar, but these are only produced when the barley grain germinates. So, barley is dampened and allowed to germinate before being dried and stored for use as malt. The starch inside the malt is still unaffected, so the first stage in beer making is to grind up the malt with water. This process allows the starch to be turned into sugar by the enzyme in the malt.

Next, the mixture is boiled to stop the enzyme working and filtered to remove any unwanted bits. Hops are then added to the filtered mixture to give the beer flavour and stop any bacteria growing.

Many years ago, beer barrels were made of wood and were hand-crafted by men called 'coopers'. Nowadays most beer is stored and transported in barrels made of aluminium.

Yeast is added to the mixture and fermentation takes place for 5–10 days. After this time the beer is put into bottles or barrels and is ready to drink.

In some parts of South America and the Middle East human saliva is used to turn the starch in grains into sugar. Indians in South America make a corn beer by chewing grains of corn and spitting them into a vessel where they undergo a spontaneous fermentation to become beer.

Hops and barley – the two main ingredients used in beer making.

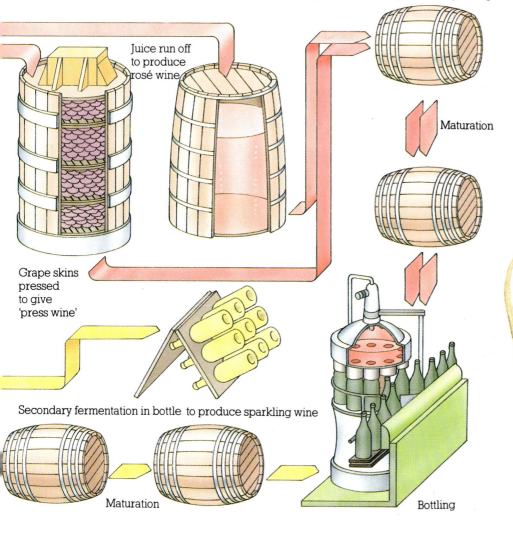

Juice run off to produce rosé wine

Maturation

Grape skins pressed to give 'press wine'

Secondary fermentation in bottle to produce sparkling wine

Maturation

Bottling

4: MEDICINES

Biotechnology has been with us for many years in the shape of antibiotics such as penicillin, and vaccines against a number of infectious diseases such as measles, diphtheria and whooping cough. In the very near future, the impact of biotechnology in medicine is going to be even greater. Rapid steps are also being made in the diagnosis of diseases. Hopefully in a few years treatments for cancers and heart diseases will be improved.

Smallpox was a painful, ugly and often fatal disease. The scarring rashes it caused can be seen on the bodies of these two young children in Bangladesh.

Prevention and Cure

Antibiotics

An infectious disease is one that can be transmitted from one person to another. Many infectious diseases, such as typhoid and cholera, are caused by bacteria.

Antibiotics work by killing bacteria and so stopping the spread of infectious diseases. Penicillin kills bacteria by stopping them from building proper cell walls. Other antibiotics work in different ways. For example, streptomycin stops bacteria from making proteins and so kills them.

Penicillin was the first antibiotic discovered and has been used for many years. Unfortunately some types of bacteria that were once easily killed by penicillin have now become resistant to it. This means that the bacteria have changed in some way, or **mutated**, so that the penicillin can no longer kill them. In some respects, this is a naturally occurring form of genetic engineering, and this kind of selection forms the basis of what Charles Darwin long ago called 'survival of the fittest'.

Resistance to antibiotics is a big problem, so new antibiotics have to be found or old ones altered in some way so that they work again. This is where biotechnology comes in. Using the techniques of genetic engineering we can develop modified antibiotics that are effective.

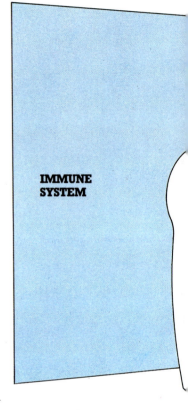

INFECTION

IMMUNE SYSTEM

OUTCOME

Vaccines

Vaccines have been one of the greatest successes in medicine. They give us the means to control some of the world's most terrible diseases. Smallpox is a good example of this. In 1967 over 10 million people were infected with smallpox. Today, it has been completely eradicated. Many other diseases can be prevented by vaccines including polio, rabies, yellow fever and rubella (German measles).

All these diseases have one thing in common: they are caused by viruses. Viruses are intracellular parasites – tiny structures that can reproduce themselves only inside living cells.

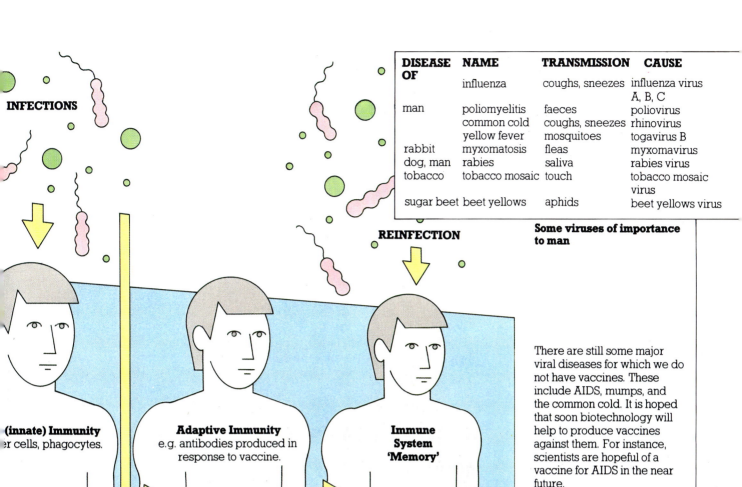

INFECTIONS

DISEASE OF	NAME	TRANSMISSION	CAUSE
	influenza	coughs, sneezes	influenza virus A, B, C
man	poliomyelitis	faeces	poliovirus
	common cold	coughs, sneezes	rhinovirus
	yellow fever	mosquitoes	togavirus B
rabbit	myxomatosis	fleas	myxomavirus
dog, man	rabies	saliva	rabies virus
tobacco	tobacco mosaic	touch	tobacco mosaic virus
sugar beet	beet yellows	aphids	beet yellows virus

Some viruses of importance to man

REINFECTION

(innate) Immunity
er cells, phagocytes.

Adaptive Immunity
e.g. antibodies produced in response to vaccine.

Immune System 'Memory'

There are still some major viral diseases for which we do not have vaccines. These include AIDS, mumps, and the common cold. It is hoped that soon biotechnology will help to produce vaccines against them. For instance, scientists are hopeful of a vaccine for AIDS in the near future.

In the future vaccines against major diseases such as malaria might also be developed, but this is probably some way off.

NO DISEASE

RECOVERY

NO DISEASE or DISEASE

Vaccinations
You will have had vaccinations against different diseases. Find out which diseases you and your friends are protected against.

HOW YOUR IMMUNE SYSTEM COPES WITH INFECTION

Vaccines are made by growing viruses inside living cells in a laboratory. The viruses are then collected and either killed or severely weakened before being injected into humans. In response to these foreign particles white blood cells produce **antibodies** which attack the virus. This takes some time, but it does not matter because the viruses are harmless. If, at some later date, a fully active virus of the same type gets into the body, the body's defence system is ready to attack and kill it.

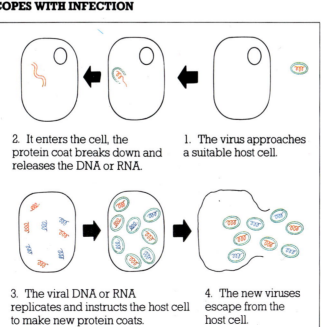

2. It enters the cell, the protein coat breaks down and releases the DNA or RNA.

1. The virus approaches a suitable host cell.

3. The viral DNA or RNA replicates and instructs the host cell to make new protein coats.

4. The new viruses escape from the host cell.

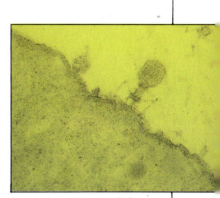

A virus on the wall of a bacterial cell, ready to enter it and reproduce.

Reproduction of a virus.

25

Genetic engineering provides the hope of producing many human hormones in reasonably large quantities so that their effects can be investigated, and diseases resulting from hormone deficiencies can be cured.

The child on the left has growth hormone deficiency. She is 1½ years older and 7 inches shorter than her sister on the right.

This graph shows the human growth curve for boys, with the normal range shown in the shaded area, and the effective treatment of a boy with much lower than average growth rate by biotechnology-produced human growth hormone.

Human Therapy

Dwarfism is one disease for which biotechnology can supply a vital missing protein such as a hormone. Dwarfism is caused by a lack of growth hormone (a hormone produced by the pituitary gland at the base of the brain). Growth hormone is vital for growth and development. A lack of growth hormone prevents children from growing to a normal height. If the lack is diagnosed early enough, these children can be given extra growth hormone (extracted after death from human donors) to help them.

However, in 1985, many countries stopped using growth hormone made in this way because a small number of children in the USA experienced severe problems. These problems were thought to be caused by an impurity in the extract.

Recently, Eli Lilly & Company successfully produced growth hormone by genetic

Growth hormone is produced by the pituitary gland at the base of the brain.

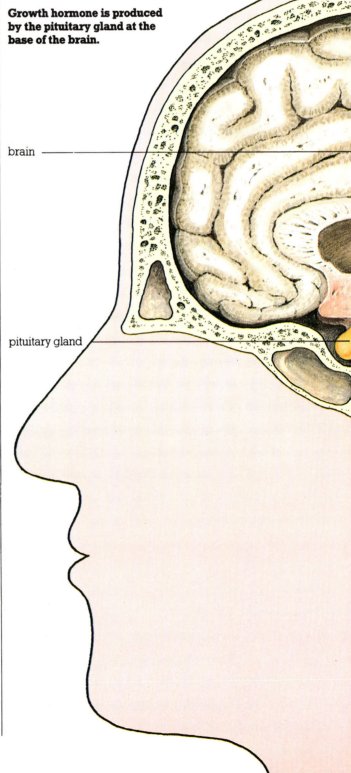

brain

pituitary gland

HUMAN GROWTH CURVE

BOYS

Height

HUMAN GROWTH HORMONE TREATMENT

cm														
190														
180														
170														
160														
150														
140														
130														
120														
110														
100														
90														
80														
70														
60														
50	1 2 3 4 5 6 7 8 9 10 11 12 13 14 15													

Age in years

engineering and already it has been used in carefully controlled clinical trials with many patients in Britain and the USA.

A single vat containing 500 litres of genetically-engineered bacteria can produce as much growth hormone as 35,000 human pituitary glands!

Once larger quantities of growth hormone are available it is hoped to test for its effects on other diseases. These include a disease of the bones due to loss of calcium called osteoporosis. Other applications could include treatment of bleeding ulcers and helping the healing of burns, wounds and broken bones.

The present sources of hormones fall into four types:

1. animals (in which case they may be different from human hormones)
2. human blood, urine or organs
3. cells grown in the laboratory and
4. chemical manufacturing methods.

Producing growth hormone by genetic engineering.

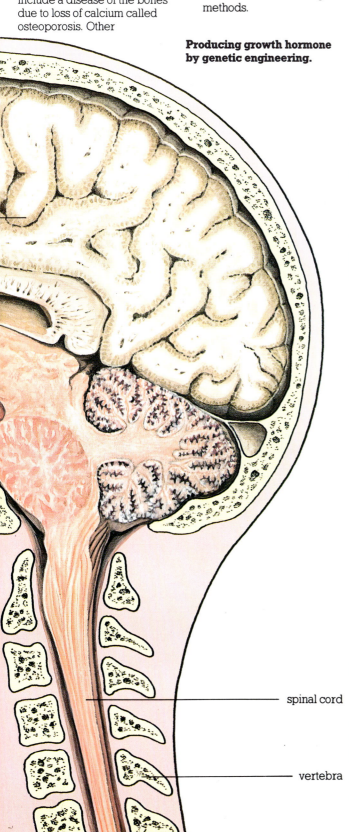

spinal cord

vertebra

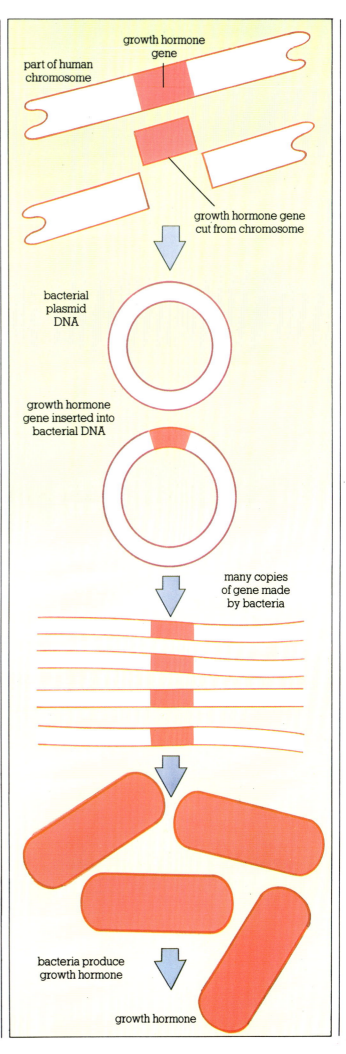

part of human chromosome

growth hormone gene

growth hormone gene cut from chromosome

bacterial plasmid DNA

growth hormone gene inserted into bacterial DNA

many copies of gene made by bacteria

bacteria produce growth hormone

growth hormone

Monoclonal Antibodies

It has long been the dream of scientists and doctors to produce a drug that could kill microbes without affecting any other cells of the body. So far no such drug can quite do that, and even the best drugs occasionally produce harmful side-effects. In 1975 scientists working in Cambridge took a step nearer the dream when they discovered how to produce substances called monoclonal antibodies.

Monoclonal antibodies are made by special cells and are proteins with the amazing property of recognising 'foreign' substances, either in the blood stream or in tissues. This means that they are useful for helping doctors to detect and treat many types of disease, and will eventually help to treat cancers in man. The special cells which make monoclonal antibodies are called hybridomas and are made in test tubes by joining a special rapidly dividing cancer cell with an 'educated' normal cell which knows which antibody to make. These hybridomas can therefore divide and multiply vigorously, producing large amounts of identical, monoclonal antibody molecules.

Diagnosis

Monoclonal antibodies can be used in the development and manufacture of new vaccines. They are made to recognise the virus protein, which the body's own defence mechanism detects, and can then be used to purify large amounts of this protein. This is

How monoclonal antibodies are made

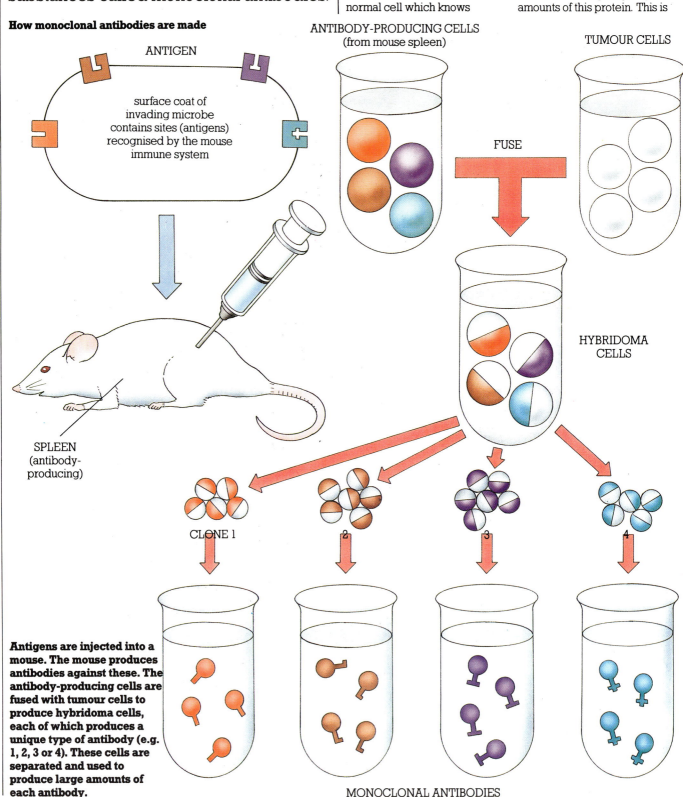

ANTIGEN

surface coat of invading microbe contains sites (antigens) recognised by the mouse immune system

ANTIBODY-PRODUCING CELLS (from mouse spleen)

TUMOUR CELLS

FUSE

HYBRIDOMA CELLS

SPLEEN (antibody-producing)

CLONE 1   2   3   4

Antigens are injected into a mouse. The mouse produces antibodies against these. The antibody-producing cells are fused with tumour cells to produce hybridoma cells, each of which produces a unique type of antibody (e.g. 1, 2, 3 or 4). These cells are separated and used to produce large amounts of each antibody.

MONOCLONAL ANTIBODIES

used to find the gene which is a blueprint for the protein and the gene is placed into a microbe using genetic engineering. The microbe then produces large quantities of the foreign protein which is the basis of new types of vaccine.

Certain types of cancer cells make abnormal proteins called 'tumour markers' which get into the blood. Once these have been identified it is easy to make monoclonal antibodies that will attach to them. Doctors then have an easier task in diagnosing these cancers and choosing a suitable treatment.

There are many other uses to which monoclonal antibodies can be put, including pregnancy testing, blood typing and the detection of rabies virus. Perhaps the most exciting use will be in the treatment of cancers. Cancer cells are sufficiently different from normal body cells that monoclonal antibodies can be made against them. Monoclonal antibodies may themselves trigger the body's defence systems to start attacking cancer cells.

Taking this idea one step further, doctors hope one day to use monoclonal antibodies as 'guided missiles' to deliver a drug straight onto the cancer cells.

Many cancer drugs produce harmful side-effects in a patient by affecting normal cells as well as cancerous ones, so it is a good idea to give these drugs in <u>small</u> doses and direct them to the site of the cancer cells. Using

this idea the doctors would not even have to know where the cancer was – the monoclonal antibody would find it for them!

Detection and combatting of disease using monoclonal antibodies is possible. Microbes, viruses, proteins and many other substances all have characteristic antigens. Monoclonal antibodies which recognise specific antigens can be linked to light-emitting molecules which shine under ultraviolet light. These antibodies are added to a sample of blood or other material taken from the patient. If the antigen is present, the antibodies will cling to it. The sample is then washed to remove unbound antibodies. Any light emitted after the washing process shows that the particular antigen and hence the microbe is present.

A possible approach to cancer treatment using monoclonal antibodies. A drug is linked to a monoclonal antibody that recognises antigens on cancer cells. When the antibody/drug package is injected into the body it will seek out cancer cells and destroy them.

Cancer cells in culture dotted with an antibody/drug combination designed to seek out a tumour.

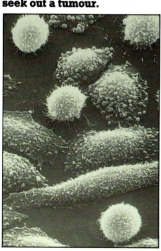

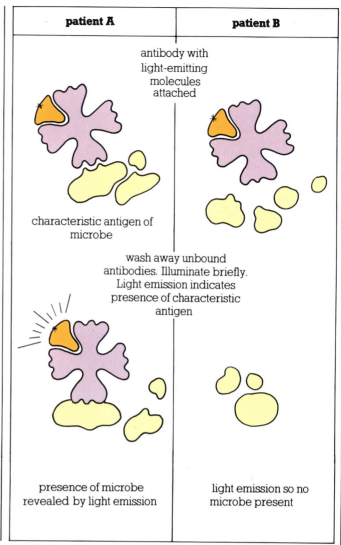

patient A	patient B
antibody with light-emitting molecules attached	
characteristic antigen of microbe	
wash away unbound antibodies. Illuminate briefly. Light emission indicates presence of characteristic antigen	
presence of microbe revealed by light emission	light emission so no microbe present

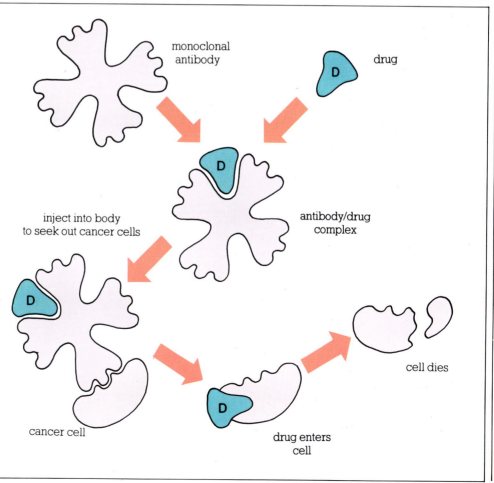

monoclonal antibody

drug

antibody/drug complex

inject into body to seek out cancer cells

cancer cell

drug enters cell

cell dies

Hopes for the Future

Cancer and heart disease kill over half the population of the developed world. Biotechnology will be a key tool in the prevention, diagnosis and treatment of these diseases in years to come. Though major problems remain to be overcome there is hope on the horizon.

Heart attacks take place when the blood vessels supplying the heart become blocked. This may come about for a number of reasons. But if the blockage is caused by a blood clot, a naturally occurring chemical 'unblocker' which has been produced by genetic engineering could come to the rescue. This compound works by stimulating components of the blood to break down the clots and clear the blockage. In the near future this biological pipe cleaner could come into general use and save many lives.

Cancer is the other major killer in the developed world. Monoclonal antibodies can help in the detection and treatment of some cancers and will be used in the future as precise labels to direct drugs straight to the site of cancer cells.

Another big hope for the treatment of cancers is the substance **interferon**, an important component of the body's own immune system.

Interferon was once famous for being the world's most expensive substance – costing £10 million per gram! This is because it is only present in tiny quantities in white blood cells and until recently it took thousands of litres of blood to produce just a few milligrams of interferon. But the price is falling fast because it can now be produced by genetically-engineered bacteria and mammalian cell culture. It seems that interferon is effective in certain types of cancers and viral diseases, but it will be several years and many clinical trials before we really know.

Enzyme replacement therapy provides hope for many people suffering from genetic diseases in which their bodies fail to make a vital enzyme.

Even more dramatic results have recently been described with erythropoetin. This is a natural substance produced by the kidney which stimulates the production of red blood cells in the bone marrow. Erythropoetin produced by biotechnology has been used to treat successfully the anaemia (low red cell count) that accompanies kidney failure and may be useful for treating other types of anaemia without the need for blood transfusion.

A cell culture plant used to make interferon.

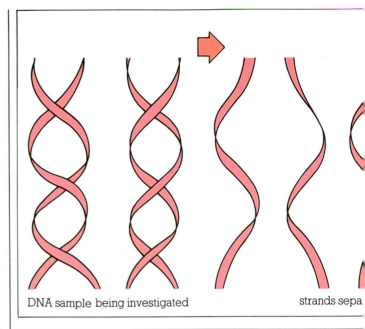

DNA sample being investigated   strands sepa

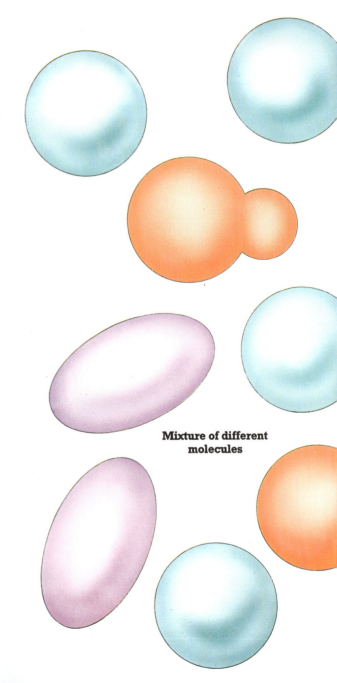

Mixture of different molecules

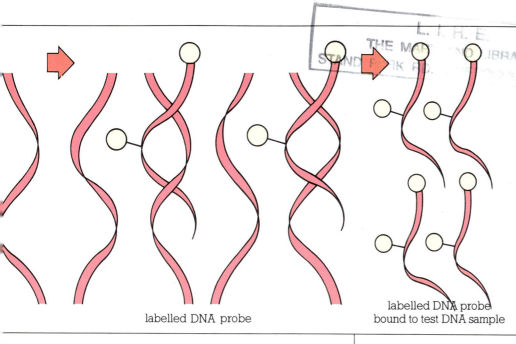

labelled DNA probe

labelled DNA probe
bound to test DNA sample

How DNA probes work.

Double-stranded DNA is extracted from the sample being investigated. Chemicals are added to separate the strands. Single strands of DNA complementary to some characteristic part of the sample DNA are introduced. These strands (the DNA probes) have previously been 'labelled' with some material that can be readily detected e.g. radioactivity. The probes attach themselves to the sample DNA in places where the sequence is complementary e.g. a particular gene. In this way the presence of, for example, a harmful or defective gene can be detected.

Detector

Transducer

Output

Biosensor

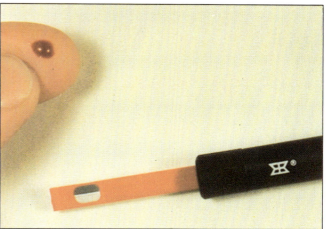

Biosensors are special devices for measuring low levels of biological materials, and will play a large role in medicine in years to come. They will enable scientists to diagnose rare diseases, or small quantities of substances in the blood or in cells. For example, a biosensor that detects levels of glucose in the blood could be coupled to a special insulin infusion pump worn by diabetics. In this way the correct concentration of insulin could be maintained in the blood without the diabetic needing an injection every day.

How biosensors work.

Biosensors can pick out very low levels of particular chemicals by joining together a biological detector with a **transducer**. In this way, when the chemical we are looking for collides with the detector an electrical signal is produced. This can be amplified (made larger) so that it is easier to see.

The new biosensor that can detect levels of glucose in the blood.

DNA probes, which have grown out of genetic engineering research, may turn out to be more effective than monoclonal antibodies for diagnosing diseases. DNA probes are short pieces of DNA that can be designed to stick very specifically to other pieces of DNA. For example, they can be used to find out whether a patient's blood contains the DNA of a certain type of bacterium or even if the patient has a genetic defect. The possibilities are enormous.

Genetic Fingerprinting

Recently a British laboratory has discovered patterns in the DNA that are unique to each individual, allowing so-called 'genetic fingerprinting' to help the police solve crimes and establish family relationships.

Around 2800 different diseases are known to be caused by a defect or mutation in just one of the patient's genes. And about one in ten people have or will develop an inherited genetic disease. Some of these genetic diseases are quite common – cystic fibrosis, which affects the lungs, is found in one out of every 2500 babies born in Britain.

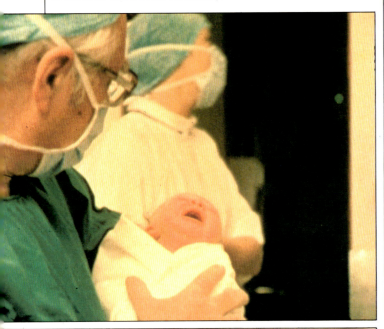

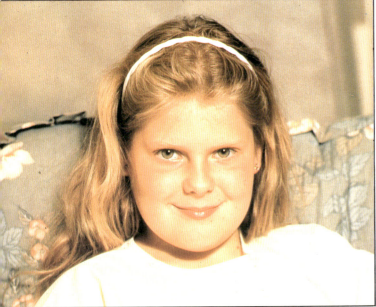

Fiction and Reality

Each of us carries about half a dozen defective genes. We remain quite unaware of this fact unless we, or one of our relatives, are amongst the many millions of people who suffer from a genetic disease.

There is no need to panic! Most of us do not suffer any harmful effects, because we carry two copies of nearly all our genes – one from our mother, the other from our father.

When a disease is caused by the lack of just one special protein, we can try to replace that protein and so cure the disease. For example, we can cure diabetes by giving insulin.

Test Tube Babies

Some married couples have trouble producing a baby. This can be because of problems with either the man's or the woman's reproductive system. In recent years doctors have developed a technique to help these people, called *in vitro* fertilisation. *In vitro* means 'in glass' and describes how an egg can be removed from the mother's body and stored under special conditions in the laboratory. It is then fertilised with sperm taken from the father. The process of fertilisation takes place outside

Louise Brown, the world's first 'test tube baby'. Louise was born in 1978. She was delivered by Mr Patrick Steptoe, who, with Dr Robert Edwards, pioneered the test tube baby technique in Cambridge. It is now used around the world. The technique has allowed many couples, previously unable to have children, to have healthy, normal babies.

Louise on her tenth birthday.

the mother's body and though the term 'test tube baby' has been used to describe this procedure it does not in fact take place in a test tube, but rather in special shallow dishes in which sperm and egg are mixed. The newly fertilised egg is then replaced in the mother's body where it grows normally to produce a healthy baby.

Gene Therapy

Another possible technique for treating diseases that are due to a single gene defect is gene therapy. In gene therapy, a faulty or absent gene is replaced with a correct gene. This eliminates the cause of the disease, and the body can then make the necessary protein.

The only attempts at gene therapy in humans, so far, took place in 1980. Unfortunately these did not work.

Doctors' and scientists' understanding of how genes work has progressed since then and the time when gene therapy will be used successfully is not far away. The first cases will probably involve replacing genes in bone marrow cells because these genes are the easiest to work with.

1. Somatic gene therapy 'Scientists interfere with Nature' was a common newspaper headline that greeted the earliest discussions of gene therapy. This happened because people did not really understand the technique: they thought that the 'new' genes could be passed on to the patient's children. In fact this was impossible because the type of gene therapy being used was *somatic gene therapy* and involved cells of

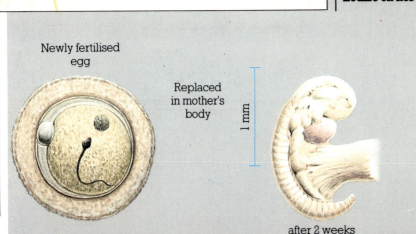

Newly fertilised egg

Replaced in mother's body

1 mm

after 2 weeks

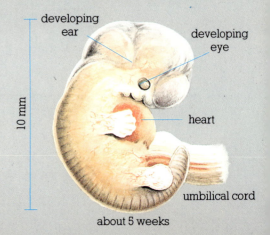

developing ear

developing eye

10 mm

heart

umbilical cord

about 5 weeks

the body that have nothing to do with reproduction.

2. Germline gene therapy
Another type of gene therapy called germline gene therapy, could, however, involve cells that are concerned with reproduction – the sperm cells in males and the egg cells in females.

Germline gene therapy is much more controversial than somatic gene therapy. It raises many moral and ethical questions because it affects not only the individual it is performed on, but also his or her descendants.

There are arguments both for and against germline therapy. Some people say it should be allowed because it offers the chance of getting rid of serious diseases in man which would otherwise be passed on to the next generation. Others argue that germline therapy would change the genetic 'pool' of the entire human species and future generations would have to live with that change, for better or worse.

But all these arguments may just be discussion topics because it is unlikely that germline therapy will be attempted on human embryos. This is because, at present, the technique is unpredictable and may cause changes in the body other than those expected.

From test tube to baby:
stages in the development of the human embryo.

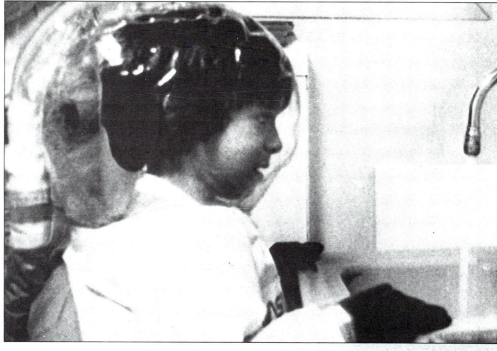

Scientists are working on these problems using animal embryos. Using a number of different techniques they can produce adult animals that sometimes bear the foreign gene in some or all of their cells. For example, scientists have been able to inject the genes for human growth hormone into mouse eggs. These genes produced three times the normal amount of protein hormone in the blood and the mice grew to twice their normal size. Research work in this area may eventually lead to new

approaches to the treatment of human growth defects.
Using germline therapy to change the characteristics of humans is the aspect of gene therapy that is most controversial. In the distant future scientists may be in a position to alter human intelligence or physical characteristics. But should they be allowed to?

David, the 'Bubble Boy', who had to live in a special germ-free suit because he had no immunity to disease. Here he watches in amazement after turning on a tap for the first time in his life at age six. David died in 1984. It is hoped that gene therapy might be used to treat this rare condition.

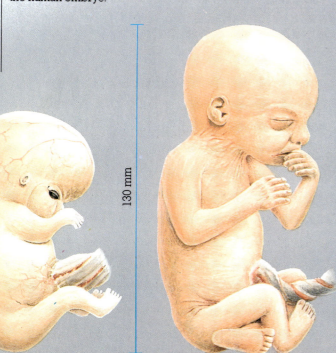

130 mm

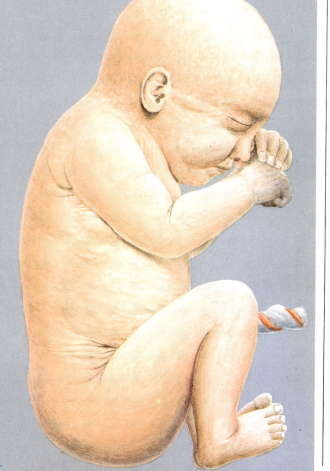

390 mm

8 weeks

5th month

9 months, a few weeks before birth

5: PRODUCTION

Penicillin was the first antibiotic to be discovered and is also the best known. It was the need for large quantities of penicillin during World War II that triggered the start of the antibiotics industry. Since that time the industry has grown to its present massive scale. The antibiotics produced by this industry have saved many millions of lives.

Scaling Up

Anyone who has ever tried to make beer in their airing cupboard at home will have a fairly good idea of the problems that face a biotechnologist in industry. To make a good quality beer you need to pick the right ingredients and the right yeast. The fermentation must be carried out in the right sort of container, kept at the correct temperature and protected against contamination. Compared with the problems of keeping one of today's industrial fermentation processes sterile, the homebrewer's problems are tiny.

For an industrial process to make a profit, biotechnologists have to solve a number of problems. Assuming they have got the right microbes (which they may have genetically engineered) they have to find the right nutrients on which to feed them. They have to design and build a fermentation system that works, and work out a suitable fermentation time to produce the maximum amount of product. They must also work out ways of separating and purifying the product so that it does not cost too much!

When a fermentation is carried out in a bucket or a small laboratory fermenter it usually looks after itself with no further help from a brewer or biotechnologist. Often, however, it may need to be shaken to help air get in and so encourage the growth of the yeast.

On a laboratory scale the amount of surface area of beer exposed to the air is sufficient to let enough air in and heat

How penicillin is produced.

1 The first stage in penicillin production is to make a broth of spores from the penicillin-producing mould.

2 This broth is fed into the production fermenter, where nutrient and oxygen supply are carefully controlled at the optimum condition for growth. Under these conditions, the mould cells multiply rapidly, doubling their mass every 6 hours. After about 40 hours, the cells begin to produce penicillin. They may continue producing it for anything up to 160 hours. After this time the fermentation process is complete. The fermentation vessel is full of a thick broth of microbial cells, as well as some unused nutrients and the dissolved penicillin.

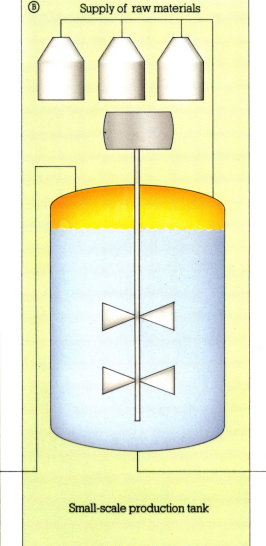

Supply of raw materials

Small-scale production tank

Production fermenter containing sterilised nutrients

Penicillin Production
Ⓐ Culture Stage
Ⓑ Seed Stage
Ⓒ Fermenter Stage

Culture of inoculum.

deep-frozen living cells

Ⓐ

Broth containing dividing cells

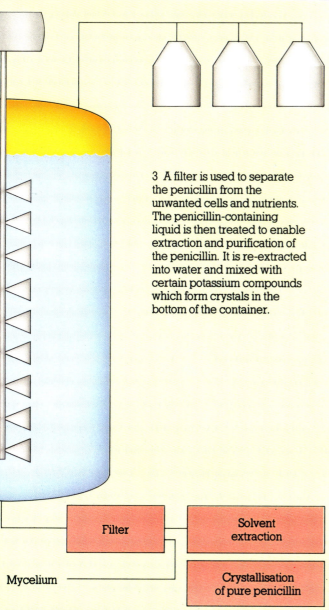

3 A filter is used to separate the penicillin from the unwanted cells and nutrients. The penicillin-containing liquid is then treated to enable extraction and purification of the penicillin. It is re-extracted into water and mixed with certain potassium compounds which form crystals in the bottom of the container.

Mycelium

Filter

Solvent extraction

Crystallisation of pure penicillin

out. Sterilisation of the system is quick and easy.

The scale-up problems in increasing from the size of a laboratory fermenter of 10 litres volume to an industrial one of 20,000 times the size are huge.

There are three great differences between this large-scale fermentation and the tests in the laboratory:

1. The ratio between the volume of the fermenter and its surface area has changed so much that the heat produced by fermentation cannot escape and the fermenter slowly heats up. This heat could eventually kill the microbes in the fermenter.

2. The amount of oxygen (supplied as sterile air) that can get to the microbes in the middle of the fermenter is reduced. This can slow down the growth of the microbes. Also, this lack of oxygen could encourage the growth of unwanted microbes which could wreck the fermentation.

3. The problem of sterilisation is much greater.

When a fermentation is over the valuable product must be removed and separated from unwanted wastes, sometimes the most difficult and costly part of the process. This is often done by filtering, extraction and drying. The product is now ready for further microbial or chemical modification and purification before it goes off to be packed and distributed to where it is needed.

Clearly the transition from laboratory to industrial scale can be both difficult and expensive.

Antibiotics for Every Man and Every Disease

Today there are over 100 antibiotics available for use in man. This may seem a large number but really it is only a fraction of the 5000 compounds that microbes produce that can kill or disable other microbes. Some of these are too expensive to produce, whilst others duplicate the action of antibiotics we already have.

Worldwide antibiotic production is made up of four major classes of antibiotics accounting for sales of about £14 billion. These antibiotics are all superb examples of biotechnology.

Let's look at the production of penicillin as a typical example of an antibiotic produced by industry. Penicillin is produced in fermenters ranging in size from 40,000 to 200,000 litres. Before the fermentation can start the fermenter is sterilised with high pressure steam.

A flow chart for penicillin production is shown in the diagram.

● The inoculum is the first step in production and consists of a broth containing spores of penicillin-producing mould. After these spores have divided a number of times, the production culture is ready.

● In a typical penicillin fermentation the growth phase lasts about 40 hours. During this time the mould doubles in mass every 6 hours. It is during the growth phase that the greatest mass of cells is formed.

● The broth in which the cells grow contains nutrients such as yeast extracts, sugars and a source of nitrogen.

● The oxygen supply during the growth phase is critical. As the broth of cells gets thicker less oxygen can get through to each cell, so the oxygen supply is carefully monitored.

● During the penicillin production phase, penicillin is actually produced. This phase can last up to 160 hours. At the end of this phase the fermentation process is complete and the fermentation vessel is full of a thick broth of microbial cells. It also contains some nutrients that have not been used and the dissolved penicillin.

● A filter is used to separate the penicillin from the unwanted cells. The penicillin-containing liquid is then treated to enable extraction and purification of the penicillin. It is re-extracted into water and mixed with certain potassium compounds which cause the formation of crystals of penicillin in the bottom of the container. These can then be easily collected.

Penicillin
Have you or your friends ever taken penicillin? Why were you given it? Did they take it for the same illness? Find out some names of other antibiotics.

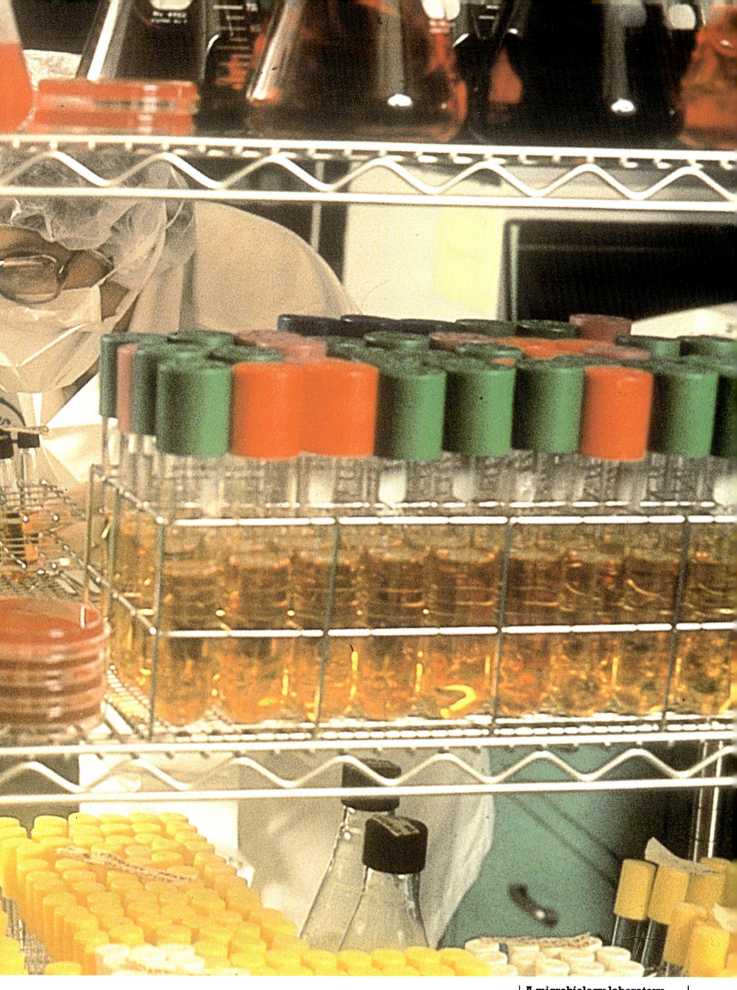

A microbiology laboratory.

Chemicals and Minerals

During World War I both Britain and Germany needed to make chemicals for use in explosives. Britain needed to make acetone whilst Germany needed to make glycerol. Both countries used microbes. When the war was over, it was found that these chemicals could be made more cheaply from oil and so production by microbes stopped.

How xanthan gum is used to recover oil. Water containing a detergent-like material is first pumped into the ground to loosen the oil clinging to rock particles. Water thickened with xanthan gum is then pumped in to act as a piston, pushing the oil-bearing mixture towards the oil well.

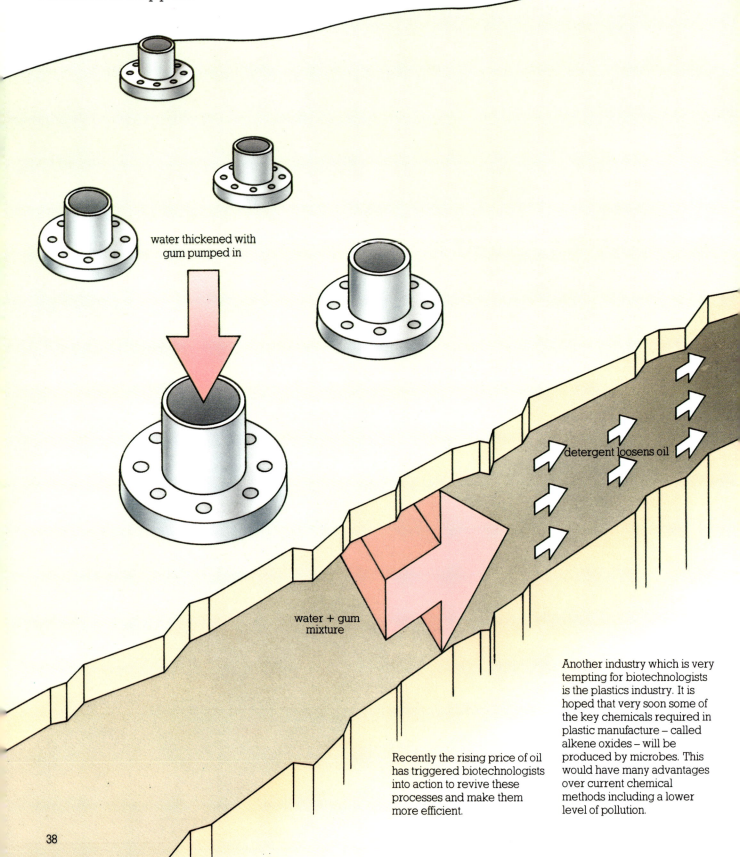

water thickened with gum pumped in

detergent loosens oil

water + gum mixture

Recently the rising price of oil has triggered biotechnologists into action to revive these processes and make them more efficient.

Another industry which is very tempting for biotechnologists is the plastics industry. It is hoped that very soon some of the key chemicals required in plastic manufacture – called alkene oxides – will be produced by microbes. This would have many advantages over current chemical methods including a lower level of pollution.

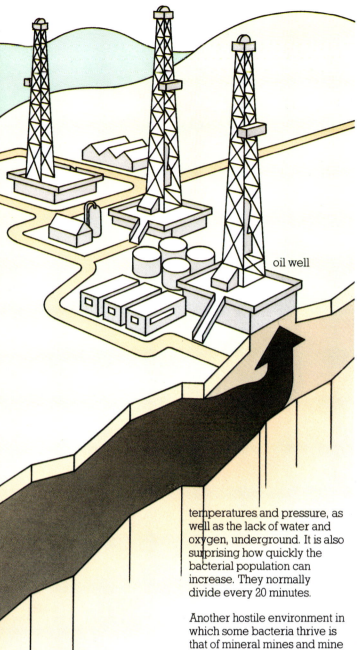

oil well

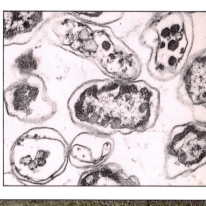

An electron micrograph showing *Thiobacillus ferrooxidans*, one of the bacteria which can cause the leaching of iron.

Some bacteria which live in mines cause the production of sulphuric acid. This dissolves metals such as iron, which results in the brown-orange colour of the water shown here. Few plants and animals can survive in this water.

Using bacteria to extract copper.

Biotechnology will help to improve the recovery of oil from the ground. When a driller first strikes oil it gushes. Unfortunately, less than half the oil does this. Most oil is not found in big pools under the ground, but rather as a coating on grains of rock. Water is too thin to push out this oil so something thicker is required. A sugary substance called xanthan gum is the answer: it is produced by bacteria and pumped into the ground. It very effectively removes oil from the rock and pushes it towards the oil well head (see picture).

An even better way of removing oil is being investigated. This involves pumping bacteria down the oil well and feeding them with nutrients until they divide enough to push the oil out. It is amazing that these bacteria can survive the very high temperatures and pressure, as well as the lack of water and oxygen, underground. It is also surprising how quickly the bacterial population can increase. They normally divide every 20 minutes.

Another hostile environment in which some bacteria thrive is that of mineral mines and mine dumps. Here they play a very important role in extracting valuable minerals.

For example, specialised 'rock-eating' bacteria live in copper mines. They do not get energy from the sun, but rather use minerals as a source of nutrients. In doing so they produce sulphuric acid and iron sulphate which attack surrounding rocks and dissolve out (leach) many metallic minerals.

These bacteria convert insoluble copper sulphide into soluble copper sulphate. As water runs down through the rocks, the copper sulphate is carried along and eventually collects in bright blue pools. The metal is recovered by passing copper sulphate solution over pieces of iron. The copper is deposited on the iron and can then be scraped off (see diagram).

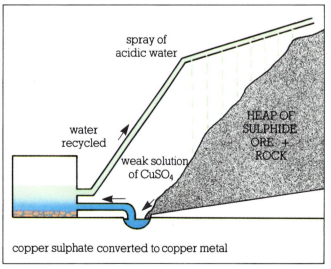

spray of acidic water

water recycled

weak solution of $CuSO_4$

HEAP OF SULPHIDE ORE + ROCK

copper sulphate converted to copper metal

Copper from copper sulphate
Take some copper sulphate solution and place in it two iron nails which are connected to a 6 volt power supply. Switch on the supply and notice the copper forming on the nails. This is called electrolysis.

Waste Management

Getting rid of rubbish is a big problem. All too often we hear about pollution caused by poor waste management – waste chemicals from factories, lead fumes in the air from cars. Biotechnology can help us to tackle these problems.

Firstly, we can use biotechnology in new production processes that are themselves less polluting than the traditional processes. For example, microbes used in the plastics industry would be fed on sugar. By contrast, when oil is used to make plastics, it can leak and cause terrible pollution, killing wildlife and ruining beaches.

Secondly, microbes can be used to 'eat up' unwanted waste and even produce something useful in the process – for example, they can produce methane from sewage. Just about every city and town in the developed world has invested in this form of biotechnology.

Most sewage works depend on the action of microbes to break down domestic and agricultural waste of various forms. Suspended solids first settle out in a sedimentation tank. Then the liquid waste is transferred to aeration tanks. Solids pass to a 'sludge digester' where bacteria break down the organic matter to a form that can be used as a fertiliser. Surprisingly, scientists still do not really understand how the microbes do this. But because they are so efficient there is little point in trying to improve the method. Instead, biotechnologists have turned their attention to dealing with other pollutants, like oil slicks.

Some bacteria thrive on hydrocarbons – the chemicals that make up oil. Unfortunately, individual strains of these bacteria can use only one or a few of the many different types of hydrocarbon. The hope is that, in the future, genetic engineers will combine the ability to use all types of hydrocarbon into a single bacterium. This one strain could then be used to clean up oil spills.

Biotechnology can be used in new production processes that are less polluting than the traditional ones.

Heavy metals, such as lead and mercury, are very dangerous to man. Lead from car exhausts is known to cause brain damage in children. Lead can be removed from petrol to reduce this risk, but it also needs to be removed from certain factory wastes.

Lead is poisonous to most microbes. But some actually go out of their way to extract lead from their environment. This strange behaviour has led scientists to the idea of growing these microbes in large pools, waiting until they have extracted the dangerous metals from their surroundings, and then collecting the microbes and disposing of them in special dumps.

Taking these ideas one step further, biotechnologists may one day be able to design special microbes to get rid of particular types of pollutants – for example a microbe to attack certain herbicides or pesticides that persist for a long time in the environment. However, not all forms of pollution can be tackled by microbes – radiation is just one major example.

This seagull has been the victim of oil pollution. Oiled seabirds like this cannot fly to reach their feeding grounds. They also poison themselves by trying to clean the oil from their feathers. Biotechnology could hold the key to dealing quickly and effectively with oil spills.

Making compost – a fertiliser
Collect leaves and waste plant material and chop up into small pieces. Pierce a large plastic bag with small holes and place a layer of the plant materials in the bottom of the bag, sprinkle on some soil and add a little water so it is moist. Carry on making layers until the bag is full – leave some air space. Tie the bag tightly and leave for a few weeks. Look at the contents from time to time. Use it on your garden!

A sewage farm works.

Car exhausts contain lead, which is very dangerous to man and known to cause brain damage in children.

6: ENERGY

Energy is the property of a system that enables it to do work. The several different forms of energy – heat, chemical, radiant and kinetic energy – can be converted into each other under appropriate conditions. When we see on the television or read in the newspapers about the price of energy increasing and the threat that there will not be enough energy to go round in the future, it is easy to forget that there is enough energy in our surroundings to meet all our possible needs. The problem is that we do not yet have the right technologies to harness this energy.

Using techniques of biotechnology, we already produce energy through fuel alcohols and methane gas. In the future, we may use biotechnology to produce hydrogen gas as well.

How Microbes Produce Fuels

Instead of putting petrol in their cars Brazilian motorists power their cars on alcohol made from sugar cane. For a small cost motorists can have their car engines modified to run on alcohol. Motorists can also run their cars, with no need for modifications, on a mixture of alcohol and petrol called gasohol. Other countries may follow Brazil's example. However, this is currently a very expensive process, as are many sources of alternative energy currently being evaluated, most of which depend ultimately on the price of oil.

Another possible large source of energy is methane, made from waste materials such as sewage. Several experimental factories are already in operation and produce methane in a two-stage process that involves both algae and bacteria.

The raw material (sewage) is fed into shallow open pools in

A Brazilian motorist filling up his car with alcohol made from sugar cane.

which algae are growing. The algae are harvested from time to time and fed into a digester which contains bacteria that feed on the algae and produce methane gas. Almost any type of plant can be fed into these methane digesters. It has even been suggested that certain types of very fast-growing seaweed could be grown on vast floating grids in the oceans. There would be many practical problems to overcome before this could be

Looking to the future: a floating seaweed farm.

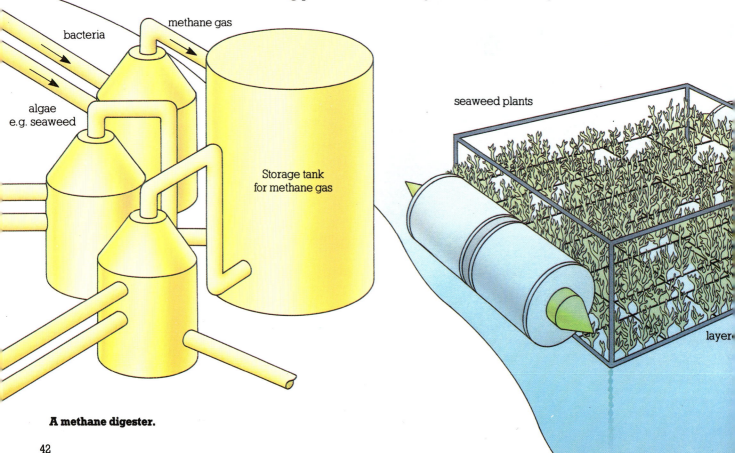

methane gas

bacteria

algae e.g. seaweed

Storage tank for methane gas

A methane digester.

seaweed plants

layer

done. For example, how would the seaweed be harvested and transported back to land, and what would happen during storms?

Recently, a technique has been developed for growing algae on land in see-through reactors (photobioreactors). Harnessing the sun's energy, the algae can be encouraged to produce a variety of useful chemicals, including oxygen and fatty acids.

The principles underlying a complex industry can sometimes provide a simple solution to a problem in a developing country.

In the People's Republic of China it is thought that there are about five million simple digesters in rural areas. In India the government's ambitious plans have already brought tens of thousands of cow dung digesters to small villages, providing cheap energy. This type of biotechnology is best suited to small-scale operations in which the raw materials are collected locally and the power produced distributed within the same area. As these digesters are very simple the difficulties found in high-technology industries can be avoided.

An exciting prospect for the

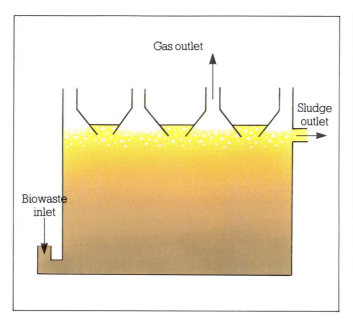

Sugar beet – a plant which might be used for the production of fuel alcohol in the future.

A simple digester.

future is the production of hydrogen gas as a fuel using biotechnology. Hydrogen would be an ideal fuel because it could be produced from a power supply that will last for many millions of years (the sun) and a raw material that covers nearly three-fifths of the globe (water). Hydrogen causes no pollution when burned, but forms water – so renewing the raw material.

There are a number of possible ways in which hydrogen could be produced, all of which involve either microbes or plants, but there

are technical difficulties which must be first overcome before hydrogen production on a large scale can become a reality. Even so, using biotechnology, there is hope for the future.

Renewable Sources of Fuel
One of the great challenges of biotechnology is to try and improve upon natural processes such as alcoholic fermentation so that the yield of alcohol is increased and the process made as efficient as possible. This would represent a move away from fossil (non-renewable) fuels such as coal, petrol and oil on which we depend at present. We must plan now for the time when fossil fuels are depleted.

For the yeast cells, alcohol is an unwanted by-product of fermentation. Indeed, alcohol can be positively harmful to yeast if the concentration gets too high. The yeast stops growing and may even die. A large proportion of the production cost of the alcohol arises from the need to purify the alcohol from the dead yeast cells in the fermentation vessel. Normally the mixture is heated so that it boils and a vapour is given off containing fairly pure alcohol. This requires a lot of heat. The process would be simpler if there was more alcohol in the vessel in the first place. Biotechnologists are working on finding, or producing by genetic engineering, better

strains of yeast that can stand higher concentrations of alcohol and so save production costs.

It is important to do this because fuel alcohol produced in this way must compete with other types of fuel, and also with alcohol produced by purely chemical processes.

In Brazil, their National Alcohol Programme produces nearly five billion litres of alcohol per year, mainly from sugar cane juice. In America, corn is used. But both these crops have a high food value. It is a matter of debate whether they should be used to produce fuel or food.

To solve this ethical problem biotechnologists are searching for other plants from which to make fuel. Since humans do not usually eat trees and grasses these would be ideal for producing fuel alcohol from. Unfortunately, yeast cannot use the cellulose part of plants (cellulose surrounds all plant cells, giving them strength), but some moulds can. It is hoped that by using genetic engineering biotechnologists can put the genes from moulds into yeasts so that the yeasts can produce the enzyme cellulase which digests cellulose. These new yeasts would then be able to produce fuel alcohol from almost any type of plant material or even industrial wastes such as those from paper-making factories.

Alcohol from plants
Mix chopped apples, water and yeast together in a conical flask, attach a bung and delivery tube (why?) and leave for about a week. Smell the contents. How would you separate the alcohol formed from the mixture?

7: IN PRACTICE

Biotechnology in practice is not without its problems. Experiments in genetic engineering must be carefully controlled to ensure the balance of nature is not upset. Following the development of a new product – for example a medicine – in the laboratory, there are the problems of scaling up and extensive testing before it can be put on the market.

IN an unprecedented move, the National Academy of Sciences has called for a voluntary worldwide moratorium to be placed on an area of scientific research because of potential and unpredictable hazards to human health. A statement drawn up by a committee of eminent biomedical scientists and released by the academy this week calls for a temporary halt on two types of genetic engineering research because of the risk of infecting man with bacteria containing hybrid DNA molecules whose biological properties cannot be predicted in advance.

The academy is concerned about experiments which combine fragments of DNA from different sources to form a hybrid molecule which can then replicate in bacteria such as E. coli, which is normally present in the human intestine. The Committee on Recombinant DNA Molecules, whose members* have all agreed individually to renounce two types of experiments involving such techniques until the potential hazards have been evaluated, has called for a committee to be established to define the hazards and to develop guidelines under which such research should be conducted. Part of the statement is given here.

*PAUL BERG, Chairman; DAVID BALTIMORE, HERBERT W. BOYER, STANLEY N. COHEN, RONALD W. DAVIS, DAVID S. HOGNESS, DANIEL NATHANS, RICHARD ROBLIN, JAMES D. WATSON, SHERMAN WEISSMAN, NORTON D. ZINDER.

Stepping Carefully

In 1974, Paul Berg wrote a letter to the science journal *Nature*. The letter was also signed by other well-known scientists and called for a ban on all genetic engineering experiments.

Berg wrote the letter because he was afraid of the consequences of a leak (or escape) of genetically-altered organisms from a laboratory into the environment.

In response to the letter, genetic engineers all over the world stopped work until new sets of rules governing genetic engineering experiments could be set up.

This letter caused much debate amongst scientists, politicians and the public. As a result, special committees were set up to monitor genetic engineering experiments, and to stop the ones they thought too dangerous.

In some countries, such as Japan and the Netherlands, genetic engineering experiments were banned altogether. In other countries, such as Britain and the USA, experiments had to be carried out in specially built laboratories in order to prevent the escape of the microbes.

One of the main reasons for concern was that the bacteria used for many experiments, *Escherichia coli*, is found naturally in the human gut. People were worried that genetically-altered *E. coli* could escape and cause widespread disease.

It was proposed that microbes used in genetic engineering experiments should be

genetically 'crippled' – that is altered so that they could not live outside the laboratory anyway. This was done in many cases.

A few years passed and it was shown that most genetically-altered microbes could not live outside the laboratory anyway because they needed special conditions to survive. These included a very complicated mixture of nutrients. It was also discovered that swapping of genetic material took place naturally between certain microbes with no harmful consequences.

Gradually the rules controlling genetic engineering and the use of genetically-engineered organisms in Britain and around the world were relaxed. In 1985 the Organisation for Economic & Cultural Development (OECD) issued a set of recommendations to its 24 member nations dealing with

environmental, industrial and agricultural applications. These recommendations have been used by the UK Government as the basis for its Guidance. The European Commission are in the process of producing rules which will cover all of the European Community.

It is now believed that the public in general is not at risk from genetically-engineered microbes. There is some concern, however, about people working in biotechnological industries who are exposed to such microbes. This is mainly because some people have become allergic to certain microbes – in other words they become ill if exposed to them, just as people with hay fever

are allergic to grass pollen. Industries are now taking special precautions to prevent this happening.

Recently there has been much debate about whether or not

special genetically-engineered viruses that can kill crop pests should be released into the environment. The debate is still continuing. What do you think?

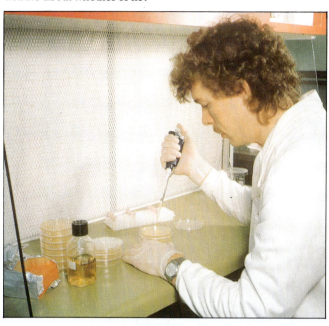

A scientist putting bacteria onto nutrient medium (agar) in petri dishes. The work is being carried out in a special sterile cabinet.

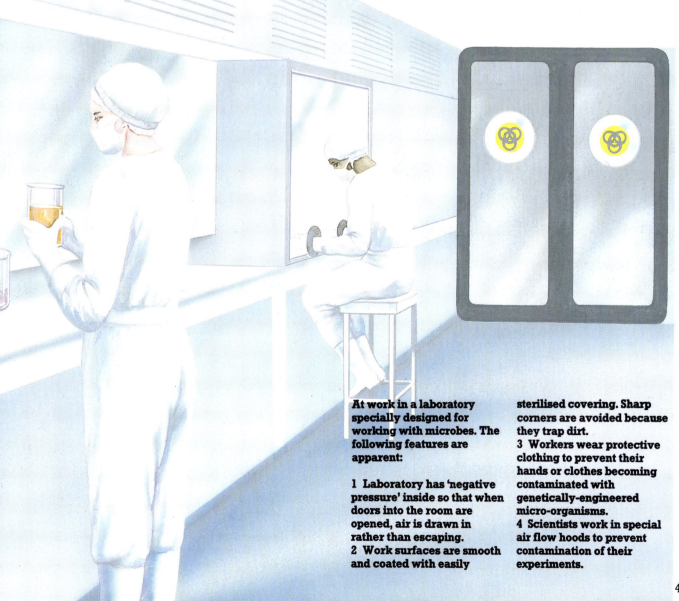

At work in a laboratory specially designed for working with microbes. The following features are apparent:

**1 Laboratory has 'negative pressure' inside so that when doors into the room are opened, air is drawn in rather than escaping.
2 Work surfaces are smooth and coated with easily** **sterilised covering. Sharp corners are avoided because they trap dirt.
3 Workers wear protective clothing to prevent their hands or clothes becoming contaminated with genetically-engineered micro-organisms.
4 Scientists work in special air flow hoods to prevent contamination of their experiments.**

Working in the New Industry

As our understanding of biotechnology increases, so will the number of products it produces and the number of people it employs.

From Laboratory to Patient

Once a product – for example a genetically engineered medicine – has been developed by biotechnologists it has to fulfil a number of requirements before it becomes available to us.

To prevent the idea or the method of production being copied a patent must be taken out. Next, before the medicine can be used in man it has to be tested in animals to check for any unwanted side effects. The details of these trials are submitted to a special government department which decides whether or not it is safe for humans.

The first humans to receive the drug are healthy volunteers. If it has no serious side effects in these people, it can then be tried out on sick people in very carefully controlled clinical trials. If these trials are successful the drug is licensed by the government.

This entire process can take from 10 to 15 years! Such a long time, however, is needed to make sure that the medicine is absolutely safe, whether it is for human or animal use.

The next problem to be tackled is scaling up the production process from a laboratory scale to full industrial scale production. This part of the drug's development is particularly expensive and often full of problems. The pharmaceutical company has to be sure that the market for the drug will be big enough to ensure:

1. that all the production costs are covered and
2. that enough of the drug is sold to make a profit.

Unfortunately, in the past, economic factors of this type have affected whether or not a medicine has become available. Some very serious diseases affect only a few people and because of the high cost of drug development many drug companies could not afford to produce these medicines. Hopefully, biotechnology will help to reduce development costs so that companies can afford to make such drugs. However, the main advantage is likely to be the production of a much wider range of new medicines.

In recent years many small high-technology companies working in the biotechnological field have sprung up to take advantage of this rapidly growing industry. These companies often employ only a few people, but can produce products with remarkable speed. For example, there are now at least 60 small companies in the USA alone, producing different types of monoclonal antibodies. Small companies of this type may only produce one product and are very specialised.

The Biotechnology Team

A Biotechnology team is made up of many different people with different qualifications and experience. Specialists will certainly be needed – scientists of various kinds – but these are a relatively small fraction of all those involved. Someone must build the factory, run the office, work the computers, make and repair the fermenter with all its complex electrical fittings, transport the raw materials to the site and the products to the consumer.

Further Information

Further reading

Higgins I. J., Best D. J., Jones J. (eds), *Biotechnology: principles and applications*, Blackwell Scientific (1985)

Master bakers' book of breadmaking, National Association of Master Bakers (1989)

New Scientist (weekly magazine), IPC Magazines

Museums

Natural History Museum, Cromwell Road, South Kensington, London SW7 5BD

Science Museum, Exhibition Road, South Kensington, London SW7 2DD

Organisations

Boots Co. plc, Corporate Affairs Department, 1 Thane Road West, Beeston, Nottingham, NG2 3AA

BP Research Centre, Chertsey Road, Sunbury, Middlesex TW16 7LN

British Anaerobic and Biomass Association Ltd (BABA Ltd), PO Box 7, Southend, Reading RG7 6AZ

Brewing History Society, 10 Ringstead Court, Ringstead Road, Sutton SM1 4SH

Brewing Research Foundation, Lyttel Hall, Nutfield, Redhill, Surrey RH1 4HY

Brewers' Society, 42 Portman Square, London W1H OBB

Child Growth Foundation, 2 Mayfield Avenue, London, W4 1PW

Federation of Bakers, 20 Bedford Square, London WC1B 3HF

Flour Milling and Baking Research (FMBRA), Chorleywood Road, Chorleywood, Herts WD3 5SH

ICI Group Headquarters, (External Relations Department), 9 Millbank, London, SW1P 3JF

Institute of Animal Physiology and Genetics Research, Babraham Hall, Babraham, Cambs CB2 4AT

Lilly Industries Ltd, Kingsclere Road, Basingstoke, Hants RG21 2XA

National Association of Master Bakers, 21 Baldock Street, Ware, Herts SG12 9DH

Glossary

Amino acids:
The building blocks of protein molecules. There are twenty different kinds of amino acid used to construct proteins.

Antibiotic:
A type of drug made by a microbe and used to kill or stop the growth of infections caused by bacteria or moulds.

Antibodies:
Types of proteins that react with and help destroy infections (eg bacteria, viruses) invading our bodies.

Beer and brewing:
Beer is an alcoholic drink made from fermented malt flavoured with hops. *Brewing* is the process of making beer.

Biosensors:
The powerful recognition systems of biological chemicals (enzymes, antibodies) are coupled to microelectronics to enable rapid, accurate, low-level detection of such substances as sugars and proteins (such as hormones) in body fluids, pollutants in water and gases in the air.

Biotechnology:
The use of plant and animal cells, microbes and their products to produce substances that are useful to mankind.

Cell:
The basic unit of living matter. All organisms are composed of cells.

Cephalosporins:
Antibiotics with a similar chemical structure to penicillin. They can be used to treat infections that are resistant to penicillin.

Chromosomes:
Chemical packages of hereditary information, made up of long, coiled chains of DNA. Found in the nucleus of animal, plant and mould cells.

Clone:
A population of organisms produced from a single parent cell. The individuals of a clone are genetically identical.

DNA:
Deoxyribo**n**ucleic **a**cid. The complex chemical molecule that contains hereditary information which is passed from parent to offspring.

DNA probes:
Isolated single DNA strands used to detect the presence of the complementary (opposite) strands. Can be used as very sensitive biological detectors.

Enzyme:
A type of protein that speeds up a biological process and is unchanged by it.

Gene:
A unit of heredity, composed of DNA.

Genetic engineering:
Manipulation of the hereditary molecule (DNA) of cells, usually by adding extra DNA to give the cell special properties.

Insulin:
A type of protein (known as a hormone) that is produced by the pancreas when the blood sugar level is high and instructs the liver to set to work to control blood glucose. First discovered in 1921 by Fred Banting and Charles Best, its molecular structure was worked out by Dorothy Hodgkin and Fred Sanger. The relatively common disease of *diabetes mellitus* is caused by a deficiency of insulin.

Interferon:
A protein that appears in the body during infections by viruses. It is produced by infected cells and inhibits the growth of viruses.

Methanol:
A colourless organic liquid that can be used as a raw material for making other chemicals and as a food source for specialised bacteria. The protein the bacteria make when they grow (Pruteen) can be used as edible protein for animals.

Microbes:
The smallest forms of life, including bacteria, viruses, moulds (such as yeast) and single-celled plants and animals.

Monoclonal antibodies:
The term applied to a group of *identical* antibody molecules which recognise only one type of invader (antigen).

Mutation:
A change in the hereditary material (DNA) of an organism which results in an altered physical characteristic.

Nitrogen fixation:
Conversion of atmospheric nitrogen (a gas) into nitrogen compounds (nitrates, ammonia) that can be used in plants. This can be achieved by microbes and by chemical methods.

Organism:
A living creature (plant, animal, mould, bacterium).

Pancreas:
A gland (about 15 cm long) found near to the stomach. It secretes a number of digestive enzymes and hormones including insulin.

Parasite:
An organism that lives inside or on another, different organism (called the host) from which it obtains food and protection. It is important to keep humans and farm animals free of parasites as they can make the host organism sick.

Penicillin:
An antibiotic first isolated from the mould *Penicillium notatum* in 1928 by Alexander Fleming.

Plasmids:
DNA molecules that can be inherited without being linked to a chromosome. Used as vectors to carry genes by biotechnologists from one organism to another.

Protein:
Organic compound resulting from the linking together of many amino acids. The wide range of shape and function of cells reflects the variety of protein molecules found in them.

RNA:
Ribo**n**ucleic **a**cid. A complex family of chemical molecules some of which – messenger RNA – carry a copy of the coded instructions needed to make a particular kind of protein molecule. It is a key link in the chain: DNA makes RNA makes protein.

Transducer:
A device for converting one form of energy into another. Such components are essential to the working of a biosensor.

Vaccines:
Inactivated or killed disease-causing microbes. These can be injected into the body to trigger the formation of antibodies and thus protect (or immunise) the patient so that he will not develop the disease even if infected. By modern genetic engineering, vaccines can be produced more readily.

Virus:
A minute non-cellular particle that can reproduce only in living cells.

Wine:
An alcoholic drink prepared from fermented grape juice. The yeast bloom on the grape skin converts the sugar from the crushed grapes into alcohol.

Index

Acetone, microbial production, 38
Adaptive immunity, 25
Alcohol, fuel, 8, 42, 43
Alcoholic fermentation, 22, 43
Algae
  methane production, 42
  photobioreactors, 42
Alkene oxides, 38
Amino acids, 9, 47
Amylases, 23
Animals
  chimaeras, 17
  cloning, 19
  feeds, 15
  gene transfer, 17
  hormone treatment, 16
  medical uses, 17
  parasite control, 16
  reproduction, 16, 17
  vaccination, 16
Antibiotics, 8, 11, 24, 34, 47
  see also Penicillin
Antibodies, 25, 47
  monoclonal, 8, 28-29, 47
Antigen, 28, 29

Bacterium(ia), 5
  antibiotic resistance, 24
  lactic acid, 21
Baking powder, 20
Barley, 23
Beer, 4, 9, 23, 47
Bio-industrial revolution, 8
Biosensors, 31, 47
Biotechnology, 47
  as an industry, 8-9
  employment, 46-47
  team, 47
Bread, 4, 20
Brewer's yeast, 14
Brewing, 22-23

Cancer
  interferon and, 30
  monoclonal antibodies and, 29, 30
  tumour markers, 28
Cells, 5, 6, 13, 47
Cephalosporins, 11, 47
Chain, Ernst, 11
Cheese, 4, 14, 21
Chimaeras, 16, 17
Chromosomes, 5, 6, 7, 47
Cloning, 47
  plants, 13
  sheep, 19
Compost, 41
Copper extraction, 39
Cystic fibrosis, 32

Diabetes mellitus, 11, 32
DNA (deoxyribonucleic acid), 5, 47
  'blueprint for life', 7
  double-helix structure, 6, 7
  how copies are made, 7
  probes, 31, 47
  protein transcription, 7
Drug development, 46, see also Antibiotics
Dwarfism, 26

Emphysema, 17
Employment, 46-47

Energy
  fuel-alchohol, 42, 43
  hydrogen gas, 43
  methane gas, 42-43
Enzymes, 47
  in cells, 6
  replacement therapy, 30
  in washing powder, 8
Erythropoetin, 30
Explosives, 8, 38

Factor 8, 17
Fermentation
  alcoholic, 22, 43
  industrial, 34-35
Fertilisation, in vitro, 32
Fleming, Sir Alexander, 10
Florey, Howard, 11
Food, preservation, 4
Fuel alcohol, 8, 42, 43

Gas, food from, 15
Gene, 6, 47
Gene therapy, 32, 33
Genetic disease
  enzyme replacement therapy, 30
  gene therapy, 32-33
Genetic engineering, 5, 7, 47
  biotechnology team, 47
  employment, 46
  release of organisms, 45
  risks of, 44-45
  specially designed laboratory, 45
Genetic fingerprinting, 31
Gene transfer, 17
Glycerol, microbial production, 38
Growth hormone, 26-27

Haemophilia, 17
Heart disease, 30
Hops, 23
Hormones, 26, see also Growth hormone, Insulin
Human food chain, 14-15
Human insulin, see Insulin, human
Hydrogen production, 43

Immune system, 25
  adaptive, 25
  inbuilt, 25
  infection and, 25
  memory, 25
In vitro fertilisation, 32
Industry, 46
Innate immunity, 25
Insulin, 47
  animal (pork/beef), 11
  human (genetically engineered), 7, 11
  normal pancreatic production, 6, 10
Interferon, 30, 47

Lactic acid bacteria, 21
Lead removal, 41

Malt, 23
Marmite, 14
Mercury, 41
Methane production
  in developing countries, 43
  digester, 42
  from sewage, 40, 42
Methanol, 15, 47
Microbe(s), 5, 47
  edible, 14-15

Monoclonal antibodies, 8, 28-29, 47
  as cancer treatment, 29, 30
  detection and combat of disease, 29
  production of, 28
Must, 22
Myco-protein, 15

Nitrogen
  cycle, 13
  fixation, 12, 47

Oil
  extraction using xanthan gum, 38
  spills, clean-up, 40

Pancreas, 47
  insulin production, 6, 10
  position in body, 11
Penicillin, 8, 10, 24, 47
  discovery, 10
  production, 34-35
  in World War II, 11
Penicillium notatum, 10
Penicillium roqueforti, 21
Photobioreactors, 42
Plants
  clones, 13
  disease resistance, 13
  improving food value, 12
  nitrogen fixation, 12
  protoplast fusion, 12-13
  taking shoot cuttings, 13
Plasmid, 7, 27, 47
Plastics industry, 38
Protein, 6
  myco-, 15
  single-cell, see Single-cell proteins
  transcription from DNA, 7
Protoplast fusion, 12-13
Pruteen, 15

Rennet, 21
Rennin, 21
Research funding, 9
RNA (ribonucleic acid), 7, 47

Saccharomyces cerevisiae, 20
Scaling up, 24-25
Sewage works, 40
Sheep
  cloning, 19
  transgenic, 17
Sheep/goat chimaera, 16, 17
Sherry, 22
Single-cell proteins (SCP)
  in developing countries, 15
  from brewer's yeast, 14
  from methanol, 15
  from oil, 14-15
  from waste products, 15
Smallpox, 24
Spirulina, 14, 15
Starch, fuel alchohol, 8
Streptomycin, 24
Surrogate mother, 17

Test tube babies, 32-33
Thiobacillus ferrooxidase, 39
Transducer, 31, 47
Transgenic sheep, 17

Vaccines, 24-25, 28, 47
Virus(es), 5, 47
  diseases caused by, 25
  reproduction, 25

Washing powder, 8-9
Waste management, 40-41
  oil spills, 40
  sewage works, 40
Wine, 4, 22, 47

Xanthan gum, 38

Yeasts, 5
  bread making, 20
  cheese making, 21
  fuel alcohol, 43
  wine and beer making, 22-23

PRINTED IN BELGIUM BY
proost
INTERNATIONAL BOOK PRODUCTION